Journeys of Discovery

POCKET HISTORY

Journeys of Discovery

Momentous
expeditions that
expanded the world

Joseph Cummins

PIER

CONTENTS

Behind the Veil of the Unknown

Ever since the beginning of the twentieth century, with just a few exceptions, there haven't really been many true journeys of discovery. By these I mean a voyage undertaken into a vast unknown, in large part simply to find out what's out there. Of course, it wasn't just curiosity that motivated the explorers whose adventures are recounted in this volume— they also sought profit and glory. But they never would have embarked on their perilous treks had they not been impelled by a desire to see what lay behind the veil of the unknown. 'The blue haze of distance over the scrub-covered ranges towards the coast always fascinated me', Leahy wrote in his classic book *Explorations into Highland New Guinea*. Norsemen standing in western Greenland probably saw in the distance, through the phenomenon of northern weather known as the arctic mirage, the glittering mountains of North America. The Spanish soldier Cabeza de Vaca, held an unwilling slave by Indians, nonetheless became entranced with their myriad cultures as he wandered through the American Southwest in the days before all of it was destroyed utterly by de Vaca's own people.

Even the word discovery itself—meaning to *uncover* or to *make known*—is an exciting one. One of the great pleasures of reading the stories of the great journeys of discovery collected here is to put yourself in the shoes of those doing the discovering. What would it have been like to be Captain James Cook, for instance, coming upon Maori fishing in a New Zealand bay, or to be John Hanning Speke, the great British explorer of the Victorian era as he searched for the origins of the Nile River? How would it have felt to circumnavigate the globe like Magellan, discovering, in the desolate lands near the bottom of the South Atlantic 'a very hidden strait' that led to 'a great and wide sea'?

Many of these discoveries changed the course of world history and made us who we are today, but of course they had dire consequences for entire civilisations. Death attended discovery, almost always. When the conquistadors careened through the Americas in the 1500s, they found thriving native societies—huge towns and cities, with rich and breathtaking cultures. These they destroyed, not through Spanish steel, but through Spanish diseases like smallpox, which killed Indians who did not even come in contact with the conquistadors. When the next Europeans arrived at the beginning of the eighteenth century, they found only relatively primitive bands of woodlands Indians who did not even know from where the vine-enshrouded ruins deep in their forests had come. If one ever wanted a blueprint for what might happen to humankind after the arrival of a nuclear holocaust or an indestructible virus, that would be it.

Despite this, everything all human beings are, we owe to discovery. These days we may discover who we are through running marathons or engaging in cleansing ceremonies or seeking knowledge through advanced degrees. But discovery is in our blood, we can't deny it. Everything we do is about discovery. It's risky, of course. As André Gide once wrote: 'One doesn't discover new lands without consenting to lose sight of the shore for a very long time'. But if there's one thing to be learned from the stories of discovery collected herein, it's that losing sight of the shore is the first prerequisite for finding new land, without or within.

Clash of Daring Peoples
The Vikings and skraelings in the
New World

There was land somewhere out to the west—
anyone living in the isles of the North Atlantic
with a sea eye knew it. Irish monks who had settled
in the Faroe Islands watched flocks of migrating
birds flying from the northwest every autumn,
heading south. But where had they summered?
The answer came in the eighth century when these
hermit monks sailed out into the western ocean in
their *currach*s, or skin-covered boats, looking for
complete isolation. Blown by storms, or possibly
led on by a shimmering mirage, they found a large,
uninhabited island with a forbiddingly mountainous
and icy interior, but one whose outer fringes held
deep, fish-filled fjords and verdant pastureland.

The Irish monks had at last found what they
sought—remoteness—and lived there peacefully

for more than a century, but word leaked out about the island (sometimes called Thule). Attractions included great fishing, the rich farmland, even the lengthy summers—one French chronicler of the era claimed that it was a place where, in midsummer, the sun was so bright at midnight you could easily pick lice out of your shirt.

Naturally, it was not long before the Vikings heard about the place.

The Norse

Arising out of Scandinavia in the mid-eighth century, Viking raiders quickly became the terrors of the pre-medieval world, swooping down on the British Isles, where they made it a particular specialty to pillage monasteries, but also roaming as far afield as France—where their descendants would include William the Conqueror—the Mediterranean and even Russia. However, a century later, the Vikings were less pirate raiders than invading farmers, seeking land on which to settle and raise their flocks. In 860, having heard about the island the Irish monks had settled, a Viking explorer named Floki Vilgerdarsson headed out from Norway in his *knarr*—the broad-beamed, single-sailed ship that was the mainstay of Viking travel at the time—and landed there.

Vilgerdarsson's arrival scared the sparse population of monks so much that they hopped into their *currach*s and fled, presumably back to Ireland (the Vikings had by this time taken over the Faroes). It was Vilgerdarsson who actually named the island Iceland—not a brilliant public relations stroke, but it did not matter. Land-hungry settlers soon began to arrive, and by 930 all the arable pasture was taken up by some twenty thousand inhabitants. This shortage of land leads directly to a scoundrel by the name of Eric the Red and thence, less directly, to the shores of North America.

Eric the Red and the Vinland Sagas

'There was a man called Thorvald, who was the father of Eric the Red. He and Eric left their home in Jaederen, in Norway, because of some killings and went to Iceland ...'. This is taken from the *Greenlanders' Saga*, one half—along with another tale called *Eric's Saga*—of the epic narrative known as the *Vinland Sagas*. Both were written down about two hundred years after the events described. Up until archaeological finds confirmed the Viking presence in the New World, these were all we had to go on when it came to the travels and travails of the likes of Eric the Red. 'Because of some killings' could have been shorthand for Eric's life, for his temper was always getting the better of him, at which point it would strike him as a good idea to pull out his sword and run someone through.

In the somewhat more settled Viking world of the tenth century, this was a no-no, and after slaying a man in Norway he was exiled and went with his father to Iceland, arriving around 960. But with all the rich land gone, he was forced to settle in the cold and inhospitable northwest part of the island.

A stroke of good luck brought Eric into marriage with a young woman with a wealthy father and put him in comfortable surroundings in the valley of Haukadale, but, never one to stand good fortune for very long, Eric got into a dispute and ended up killing two men. He was banished from Haukadale and then got into further trouble, so much so that he was declared an outlaw and sent packing from Iceland.

It would seem that Eric the Red was rapidly running out of room to run to but, although murderous, he was bold and he had come up with a solution. Around 900 or so, a Viking named Gunnbjorn Ulf-Krakasson had been blown off course west of Iceland and sighted, in the distance, a large, mountainous country, which he did not explore but whose existence was thereafter much speculated upon in Iceland. Eric decided now was as good a time as any to try to find the place. In the summer of 982, he set sail and discovered a large island some 300 kilometres (200 miles) west of Iceland. 'He found the land he was seeking', the sagas tell us, 'and sailed south down the coast to find out if the country were habitable there'.

'This Land Seems Worthless to Me'

The east coast of the island, with huge glaciers, was icy and forbidding, but the west was much more inviting. For three summers, Eric the Red explored its inlets and fjords. The fourth summer, he returned to Iceland, announced that he had discovered a new land and that it was called Greenland—'for he said that people would be much more tempted to go there if it had an attractive name'. Eric was a far better PR specialist than Floki Vilgerdarsson, but Greenland was also a warmer place in the first millennium—it was not until three hundred years later that the climate became as frigid as it is today (or was until the onset of global warming).

Hundreds of land-hungry settlers followed Eric to this new island; one of them, arriving in 985, was Herjolf Herjolfsson, who sold his poor farm in Iceland hoping to better himself. He must have done it on the spur of the moment, for, shortly thereafter, his son Bjarni Herjolfsson, a merchant, sailed back home from a trip to Norway to find that his father had decamped. Extremely upset, Bjarni refused even to unload his *knarr* but instead convinced his crew to sail straight away to Greenland to find Herjolf. The only problem was, the ship became lost. After sailing west for days, Bjarni sighted through the mist and fog a land that was 'well-wooded, with low hills'. This did not fit the description of Greenland, so Bjarni kept sailing. Twice more he sighted flat, forested land but refused his crew's pleadings to stop there. 'This land seems worthless to me', he told them. Finally, a gale blew Bjarni north and east, and he found himself off the shore of Greenland.

The sagas tell us that Bjarni found his father and gave up trading to become a farmer; this incurious gentleman had, however, become the first recorded European to spot North America.

Leif the Lucky

Some fifteen years went by. Eric the Red had settled down. He got married again, raised livestock on a large farm and produced four children, one of whom was named Leif Ericsson. It seems, according to the sagas, that Leif was the chosen son, as his nickname, Leif the Lucky, might imply. He was 'tall and strong and very impressive in appearance', a man who sired a child by a noblewoman and who converted to Christianity when it arrived in Greenland (although he was unable to get Eric the Red to change his pagan ways).

Like Eric, Leif was restless. He had grown up hearing the tales that Bjarni Herjolfsson told about his three sightings of the strange land to the west, stories that fed Ericsson's wanderlust. And so, around 1000, he went to Bjarni and purchased the very boat that Herjolfsson had made his voyage in. Leif then gathered a crew of thirty-five about him and twisted his father's arm to get him to come on the voyage. But on the way to the ship on the morning of their departure, Eric the Red fell off his horse. He was unhurt, but Norse superstition claimed that a fall before a journey was unlucky, so Eric begged off, supposedly telling Leif, 'I am not meant to discover more countries than the one we now live in', although this has the feel of an addition by a saga-teller adjusting history to make it a little more portentous.

In any event, Leif sailed from the harbour of Brattahlid, in southwestern Greenland, and after an unremarkable voyage found himself off a barren coast with grey glaciers tumbling down into the sea. Ericsson landed briefly but found nothing of interest and began sailing on, after naming his first landfall *Helluland*—'Slab Land'. He had probably landed on forbidding Baffin Island. Undeterred, Leif and his crew sailed southeast along the North American coast and soon came to the wooded country that Bjarni Herjolfsson had seen, which was almost certainly Labrador, in eastern Canada, a place of low hills, thickly forested—and thus Ericsson called it *Markland*, or 'Forest Land'.

Up to this point there is little doubt in the minds of modern historians as to the path Leif's voyage had traced—the *Vinland Sagas*, while exaggerated in some ways, were accurate when it came to geographic details, as befits stories told by a seafaring people for whom correct landmarks often meant the difference between life and death. As Leif coursed farther south, he passed a glorious, 55-kilometre (35-mile) long stretch of yellow sand beach with, behind it, a vast forest of black spruce spreading as far as the eye could see. This beach he dubbed *Wonderstrands* and it can still be seen today, on Labrador's coast.

Vinland the Good

Continuing on, Leif and his hardy companions sailed down the coast of North America, gazing at the profusion of trees and wondering at the vastness and silence of this land—for they had seen no sign of any human habitation at all. There is an almost *déjà vu*-like intensity to the sagas here, as if the land already existed in the dreams and imaginations of those who had ventured in search of it. Some days' sail from the wondrous yellow beaches, the tired Vikings came upon a country of temperate climate, a place where salmon filled a vast river and grass for livestock grew freely on the hills. The days and nights, the saga tells us, 'were of more even length than in either Greenland or Iceland'.

Here, in this place, on a wide point of land overlooking the sea, Ericsson and his companions landed and built rude huts in order to have winter quarters while they explored. The site of Leif's huts has been identified with a reasonable degree of certainty as L'Anse aux Meadows, at the very northern tip of Newfoundland. From there, Ericsson and his men roamed south during these relatively mild winter months and found grape-vines growing in profusion (although they may have been North American gooseberries). They decided to call this place 'Vinland the Good'.

Spring came and still there was no sign of any inhabitants. After exploring southward, the Vikings packed up their belongings, boarded their *knarr* and headed for home, retracing their route north along the coast. They had many tales to tell of this uninhabited wilderness rich in timber, grapes and pastureland. Little did they know that they had been watched all along.

'This Will Lead to My Death'

Leif returned to Greenland that summer and, for reasons the sagas do not divulge, never again explored the new world he had found. But relatives of his would make it a kind of cottage industry to go to North America. The first was his brother Thorvald, who retraced Leif's steps to Vinland in the summer of 1004, taking with him a crew of thirty men. Thorvald and his men wintered at Leif's Houses, before exploring that spring, heading southwest along the North American coast. Like Leif before them, they found attractive wooded country with rivers teeming with fish. Unlike Leif, however, they discovered one jarring sign of human life, what they took to be a 'wooden haystack cover' (probably the top of a grain-storage receptacle) on the beach of an island off the coast.

Thorvald and his men returned to overwinter at Leif's Houses once again and then set off for further exploration the next summer, this time sailing north, into Markland. They sailed until they came to a beautiful spot, a point of land that jutted out into the ocean, with deep, fish-filled fjords on either side of it. The Vikings landed and explored. Thorvald admired the view greatly and told his men he would like to build a home there. Then, walking along the beach on their way back to the ship, they found 'three skin-boats with three men under each of them', according to the sagas.

Thorvald and his Vikings immediately set upon the men, killing eight of them. However, one escaped in his boat, paddling madly out to sea.

Thus, the first encounter between North Americans and Europeans was a bloody one and things would only get bloodier. Surprisingly, instead of leaving, the Vikings—'overcome by a heavy drowsiness'—fell asleep on the beach after their slaughter was done. When one of their number shouted an alarm and they woke up, they saw 'a great swarm of skin-boats ... heading towards them down the fjord'. Thorvald told the men to race for cover behind their *knarr* as the strange men attacked. Now realising his mistake in killing the men on the beach, Thorvald told his men to defend themselves as best they could, but 'fight back as little as possible'.

The enraged men from the skin-boats fired off arrow after arrow at the Vikings, who took cover behind their shields. Then, suddenly, the attack was over and the men paddled back up the fjord. Thorvald asked if anyone were injured. No one was but him—an arrow had pierced his side. 'This will lead to my death', he said. And he was right. After he died, his crew went back to Leif's Houses, where they overwintered once more before heading back to Greenland.

'They were Small and Evil-looking'

The Vikings called the men who had attacked them *skraelings*—*skraeling* means 'savage' or 'wretch' and is a contemptuous term for someone who appears scared and weak. These men, the saga records, 'were small and evil-looking, and their hair was coarse; they had large eyes and broad cheekbones'. Or so they appeared to the frightened Vikings—and there is no record of how these Scandinavians looked to the equally scared and surprised Indians. But who were these *skraelings*? The men Thorvald killed and who later killed him were probably the woodlands Indians later known as the Montaignais. They were Algonquian-speaking, paddled skin-boats that were forerunners of birch-bark canoes, shot stoned-tipped arrows and lived in conical skin huts. They were the descendants of those hardy people who had, aeons before, crossed the Bering land bridge from Asia into North America and spread out over the continent.

In this regard, they were every bit as bold and adventurous as the Vikings who faced them on that beach, but the two groups were divided by a yawning cultural chasm, and understanding each other would become a near-impossible task— killing each other, as it turned out, was much easier. When Thorvald's Vikings returned home, the news they brought was mixed.

The new land was indeed full of pastoral riches, but it was inhabited by *skraelings* who intended to fight when provoked. Therefore, the next and probably the last major party to decide to sail to Vinland would be a large one, capable of defending itself. The *Vinland Sagas* place the number at perhaps 160 men and, this time, women as well. 'Livestock of all kinds' was brought along, including, significantly, a bull. The party set sail about 1010, led by Thorfinn Karlsefni, who was married to Gudrid, widow of Leif Ericsson's younger brother Thorstein. Also present—at least according to *Eric's Saga*—was Leif's sister, the quite formidable Freydis.

'A Hail of Missiles'

This new group arrived safely at Leif's Houses in Newfoundland in early fall and overwintered without seeing any sign of *skraelings*. One day that spring, however, a group of Indians came out of the woods, carrying packs filled with furs. It seemed that their intention was peaceful trade but, according to the *Sagas*: 'The cattle were grazing near by and the bull began to bellow and roar with great vehemence. This terrified the Skraelings and they fled ... They made for Karlsefni's houses and tried to get inside, but Karlsefni had the door barred against them'.

Neither Vikings nor *skraelings* could understand each other, but finally both sides calmed down and began to trade. The *skraelings* were particularly interested in cow's milk, trading furs for long draughts of it and, as the *Sagas* tell it, 'happily went away with their purchases in their bellies'.

Despite the peaceful outcome of this incident, Karlsefni had a palisade erected around the camp but this did not deter the Indians from trading. When they returned the following year—for it appears doubtful that these Indians, who were Algonquian-speaking and possibly of the Micmac or Beothuk tribes, actually lived in the area—they simply threw their packs over the top of the fortification and lined up for cow's milk. By this time there had been born to Karlsefni and Gudrid a son named Snorri, the first European child born in the New World.

As related in the *Sagas*, Gudrid was rocking Snorri in his cradle when a woman appeared near the hearth. Startled, Gudrid asked her who she was and she said her name was Gudrid, too. Then there was a loud shout and a crashing sound, and the woman disappeared—it was apparent to Gudrid that she had been a ghost.

The clamour outside had been caused when an Indian tried to steal a weapon belonging to one of Karlsefni's men and the man had killed the Indian. The rest of the *skraelings* fled but soon returned in force and Karlsefni led his men out to do battle against them. The fight was fierce. According to the *Vinland Sagas*:

... a hail of missiles came flying over, for the Skraelings were using catapults. [The Vikings] saw them hoist a large sphere on a pole; it was dark blue in colour. It came flying in over the heads of Karlsefni's men and made an ugly din when it struck the ground. This terrified Karlsefni and his men so much that their only thought was to flee.

In fact, this large sphere was probably a rock wrapped in skin and hurled from two poles—a favourite weapon of the Micmacs at the time—but it was enough to scatter the already frightened Vikings. The day would have been lost but for Freydis, according to the version of the story told in *Eric's Saga*. Freydis was pregnant and could not run away fast enough, so:

… she snatched up a sword and prepared to defend herself. When the Skraelings came rushing towards her, she pulled one of her breasts out of her bodice and slapped it with the sword. The Skraelings were terrified at the sight of this and fled back to their boats.

Abandoning Vinland

Whether or not it really took the intervention of one of Freydis' apparently awe-inspiring breasts to scatter the *skraelings*, it was evident to the Norse that they could not ever comfortably settle Vinland. Before the Vikings arrived both Iceland and Greenland had had only small populations, of Irish monks and Inuit hunters, respectively. Both were easily scattered. These *skraelings* were another matter.

Karlsefni and his men and women returned to Greenland the next spring, carrying with them wild grapes, timber and stories of the savages who had plagued them. Theirs was the last large expedition to Vinland, although most archaeologists think it probable that numerous small parties of Norse found their way to North America from Greenland over the next three hundred years, trading and fishing in the more northerly regions of Canada. Vinland, however, was abandoned and a sad fate awaited Eric the Red's settlements in Greenland, as well.

By the mid-fourteenth century a drop in temperatures clogged the sea lanes around the large island with ice, cutting it off from frequent supply ships from Norway (whose population had, in any event, been decimated by the bubonic plague outbreak known as the Black Death). One by one, the settlers of Greenland died, of cold and exposure, until by the mid-fifteenth century there was no one left alive.

Thereafter, the stories of the Norse, the *skraelings* and the verdant Vinland the Good would dim in memory, so much so that when Columbus sailed to what he thought were the Indies he discovered a land that he was certain no European had ever set foot in before.

CHAPTER TWO

The Coming of the Dressed People
Columbus arrives in the Caribbean

Between the time the last Norsemen left the shores of North America, probably about 1300 or so, and the morning in 1492 when three Spanish ships hove into view off a small cay in the Caribbean, there were almost certainly numerous, unrecorded first encounters between Europeans and the inhabitants of the vast New World. Between 1431 and 1486, Portugal sent at least eleven adventurous captains sailing west in search of rumoured lands, exotic and real, but records of these voyages were destroyed in a fire in 1775 and so are lost to history. Ships sailing from Bristol, in England, sought western land as early as 1480, while at the same time English fishermen (almost every historian now accepts) drew up bulging nets of cod in the rich fishing grounds within sight of Newfoundland. Surely, people of the New and Old Worlds met.

But the voyage of Christopher Columbus was to be dramatically different, both for Europeans and for the Taino Indians who stood that October morning on the beach of the island they called Guanahaní and watched boats row in from the ships with the billowing white sails with red crosses emblazoned on them. To begin with, Columbus had muscle behind him—he was backed by the sovereigns of a major European power, who intended to plunder and colonise any lands they found. Every bit as important, Columbus' voyage was documented, not just in the diaries of the great Admiral of the Ocean Sea himself, but by royal scribes who accompanied the *Niña*, *Pinta* and *Santa María* for just that purpose. Others would soon know about the voyage—not just those in Spain, but people in Europe as well. And that would mean a land rush such as the world has never seen, before or since. And for the naked Indians, watching the longboats landing in the shallows, it would mean the end, forever, of their way of life.

The Admiral of the Ocean Sea

Christopher Columbus was a stubborn and often misguided man, but a brilliant one nonetheless.

Forty years old when he arrived in the Caribbean, he had been born in Genoa, Italy, a city famous for its sailors, and had probably gone to sea by the age of ten. Having become a prominent navigator, mainly in the employ of the Portuguese, he approached the King of Portugal, John II, with a proposition that he sail across the Western Ocean in order to find a new route to the Indies, whose silks and spices were in great demand in Europe. John II, intent on finding his own sea route around Africa, turned down Columbus. The Genoese then petitioned King Ferdinand and Queen Isabella of Spain, who approved and funded the expedition, right down to agreeing to name him 'the Admiral of the Ocean Sea' if he succeeded—a title Columbus' not inconsiderable vanity demanded.

Many thought Columbus was crazy when he set sail from Palos in Spain on 3 August 1492 with a crew of ninety men in a little caravan of three ships. If so, there was method in his madness. Despite the fact that the Atlantic was a great unknown, astute navigators like Columbus had already recognised that it had two different but unvarying wind systems. One, the northeast trade winds, would push a sailing vessel across the ocean from the latitudes of the Canary Islands. The other wind system, farther north, was the southwesterly trades, which presumably would blow a mariner back from the Indies.

For the first ten days of his voyage, Columbus made record time, with the trades blowing him along for 1160 nautical miles (a nautical mile is 1.85 kilometres or 1.15 miles). Since he had expected to reach land within two weeks, he was actually alarmed at this rate of progress and lied to his crew about the speed at which the vessels were carrying them into the unknown. However, by 25 September, the *Niña*, the *Pinta* and the *Santa María*—the last was Columbus' flagship— were becalmed in the Sargasso Sea, a great watery meadow of green and yellow seaweed. Now, as the trades dropped, the crews became worried. False sightings of land occurred with some regularity and certain members of the crew vowed mutiny.

It was in this fraught atmosphere that, around 2 o'clock in the morning of 12 October, a lookout aboard the *Pinta* cried out *Tierra! Tierra!* With a distant white beach gleaming in the moonlight, Columbus tacked his ships back and forth and waited impatiently for dawn.

Guanahaní

After this remarkably uneventful crossing of the Atlantic, Columbus had arrived at an outlying island of the chain we now know as the Bahamas. There continues to be some dispute about which island it is—most historians believe that it is the Watling islands, although a strong minority are convinced it is a nearby islet named Samana Cay— but Columbus named what he immediately thought of as *his* island—his and Spain's—San Salvador.

Meaning 'Holy Saviour', it was the first of a host of Christian names placed upon the New World in what one historian has called Columbus' 'frenzy' of naming, but the Taino Indians watching in wonder as the longboats ferried the crew to shore called the low, curving island Guanahaní, a word that, quite ironically, means 'welcome' in their Arawak language. Tainos had been living in the Caribbean for 1500 years by the time Columbus arrived. They had left the coast of northern South America and migrated to the Greater Antilles and points west, finding themselves in the Bahamas around 900 AD. Over the centuries, they had pushed out the original inhabitants of the Caribbean islands, the Guantahatabeys, or Ciboneys, who had probably arrived from the southeastern United States but who, by the time Columbus landed, were few in number and living only in western Cuba.

At this time the Tainos were having trouble with the Carib Indians, who had also come from northeastern South America and who were driving them farther west. All told, in 1492 there were about four million people—all of whom spoke some derivation of the Arawak language—living in the Caribbean, so Columbus had by no means found an unpopulated paradise, nor one that was in stasis. Nor, of course, had he found the Indies, although, as he spied the people on the beach, he thought he had, for he called them *Indios*, a name that stuck.

'And Make Them Do as You Wish'

When Columbus landed on Guanahaní, the Tainos who had been watching his progress gathered around him unabashedly and stared. Columbus simply ignored them. Carrying the royal banner (others in his party brandished green flags with the letters 'F' and 'Y', the initials of the Spanish king and queen, emblazoned on them), he fell to his knees, thanked God and took possession of the island in the name of Spain. Surrounded by the inhabitants of this strange and wondrous place, Columbus had decided simply to … confiscate it, the first but certainly not the last moment of supreme European arrogance in the New World.

Having performed these rites, and after erecting a cross, Columbus finally turned to observe the Tainos. 'All those that I saw were young people', he recorded, 'for none did I see of more than thirty years of age. They were all very well formed with handsome bodies and good faces. Their hair is coarse, almost like the tail of a horse—and short. They wear their hair down over their eyebrows except for a little in the back which they wear long and never cut'. Columbus was thrilled by the fact that the Tainos did not wear clothing. 'They all go around naked as their mothers bore them, and also the women', he wrote to his patrons, King Ferdinand and Queen Isabella of Spain, continuing in a gossipy tone, 'although I didn't see more than one really young girl'.

He was even more thrilled by what appeared to be the docility of these people. They were 'friendly and well-dispositioned', he wrote. They did not appear to be a threat because, 'they have no iron'. Thus, when Columbus and his men showed the

Tainos their swords made of tempered Seville steel, 'they grasped them by the blade and cut themselves through ignorance'—although it was apparent that the Tainos had experience with warfare, since their bodies bore wounds they had received, they told Columbus by sign language, they had been in warfare with neighbouring islands.

Despite this, the Tainos were gentle and relatively trusting people, and Columbus was already sensing that these men, women and children would make good servants. 'With fifty men you could subject everyone on [Guanahaní] and make them do as you wish.'

'People of High Rank'

Of course, the Tainos were by no means the simpletons Columbus portrayed them as, for theirs was an old and highly developed civilisation. The Tainos were separated into various tribes run by chiefs, or *caciques*. In fact, the word Taino itself means 'people of high rank', and some archaeologists and historians believe that the Taino tribes themselves comprised elite ruling classes who contributed the *caciques*, warriors and shamans for the Arawak-speaking populations. The elite Tainos wore feathers and golden ornaments, were sometimes carried in litters and lived in their own compounds, in longhouses with conical roofs facing a large central plaza that was used for public ceremonies. Some of this lifestyle was borrowed from that of the Mesoamerican tribes, with whom the Tainos had cross-cultural contact. The Tainos were experienced sailors, who sailed great dugout canoes, or pirogues, carrying as many as thirty people across what is now the Gulf of Mexico. Mexican iguanas (a favourite delicacy of the Tainos) and gold jewellery for noses and ears were exchanged for tobacco and other Caribbean crops.

As in any multi-level society, some people were better off than others. The naked Indians Columbus first met on the beach of Guanahaní—an island that was probably used as a base for fishing, not for permanent habitation—were commoners, farmers or fishermen, and they may even have been the class of homeless and landless people known as Naboria, a group whom the Tainos employed as servants. Whoever they were, Columbus had his eye on them. Writing in his journal, with an eye to it being read by King Ferdinand and Queen Isabella, Columbus said: 'Our Lord pleasing, I will carry off six of [the Tainos] at my departure, in order that they may learn to speak [Spanish]'.

Hunting for Gold

Of course, despite the beauty of his surroundings, one thing Columbus was disappointed by was the lack of gold and other evidence that might hint that he was in the fabled Indies. Some of the Tainos wore little plugs of gold in their noses, but all they had to trade for the red caps and beads Columbus brought them were cotton and parrots.

On 15 October, taking six Tainos with him, Columbus left to explore a larger island to the south, 'where all these men that I am taking from San Salvador make signs that there is a lot of gold and that they wear it in bracelets on their arms and their legs and their ears and their chests ... I cannot fail with Our Lord's help to find out where it comes from'. The next island, which Columbus named Santa María de la Concepción, had no glittering yellow stones, nor did the next the Tainos directed him to, nor the next. Columbus began to wonder whether the Indians were not simply moving him along to get rid of him, for he was beginning to understand that these supposedly 'simple' people were not so simple after all. The Tainos instinctively had begun doing what tribes all over the Americas would do in future generations—try to get these persistent strangers to leave by telling them that riches lay elsewhere.

Despite himself, as he journeyed through the islands, Columbus was impressed by the beauty of his surroundings, by the virtual paradise he had stumbled into. 'Islands with lofty mountains, most beautiful and of a thousand shapes', he wrote. '[The islands] are filled with trees of many kinds and tall, and they seem to touch the sky. Some were flowering and some bearing fruit. And the nightingales were singing and other birds of a thousand kinds. There are six or eight kind of palms which are a wonder to behold …' The fish, he wrote, 'are of the brightest colour in the world, blue, yellow, red, and of all colours, and painted in a thousand ways'.

At the same time that he was marvelling at the scenery, Columbus was becoming more and more callous toward the people who inhabited this Eden. At one juncture, he sent men ashore to capture: 'seven head of women, young ones and adults, and three small children'. It was an alarming sign that he thought of the Tainos as cattle.

The Fabled Cipangu

Columbus spent two weeks exploring the Bahamas, but he never found the scent of the Indies. However, he kept on hearing from the Tainos he met of a place he thought they called Colba, or Cuba (in reality, the Taino were saying *Cubanacan*, which was a name for a place in the centre of what is now the island of Cuba). In his fervour to find gold, he thought they were referring to Cipangu, which was, as reported by Marco Polo, the Chinese name for the fabled island of Japan. Columbus said the Tainos told him that the Cipangu had a huge harbour 'full of ships and sailors both many and great'.

Finally, on 28 October, led by Taino pilots, Columbus reached Cuba, only to be grievously disappointed. The bustling harbour contained only a single dog 'who couldn't bark', as Columbus wrote sardonically. They finally located a few people and asked them who their king was.

These Indians kept pointing around the coast to the west, and so Columbus sailed along Cuba's beautiful shoreline until he reached a harbour known today as Puerto Gibara. He anchored there and sent two men inland searching for the Great Khan of Cipangu. His sailors, in the meantime, attempted to show a local inhabitant of the island how to sing the 'Ave Maria'. In a few days, his men returned, having found a large village of upwards of a thousand people, but no cities. They took cotton back with them and a plant that the Indians rolled up 'to drink the smoke thereof', but nothing else.

It is difficult to know what the Tainos thought of this restless quest on the part of the Spanish. They were not acquisitive themselves. A Spanish friar who arrived in the Caribbean in 1594 studied their religion closely and found it to be one in which songs were sung to *zemis*, or gods, whose likenesses abounded in Taino huts, carved out of wood or stone. One *zemi* was Yocahu, 'the Being of Yucca', who was their great agricultural deity. The Tainos believed that they had arisen as a people from a womb in the heavens, from a celestial mother sometimes described as a 'Mother of Waters', combining the sea, lakes and rivers. They sang a great deal—songs called *areytos*, which were songs of worship, but also songs that celebrated great events in their past.

The Tainos also placed great store in dreams. According to the Spanish friar who learned their language, shortly before Columbus arrived in

1492 two Taino *caciques*, after deliberately fasting for days, had a shared dream or vision in which Yocahu appeared and told them that they would 'enjoy their domain for only a brief time because dressed people, very different, will come to their land and will impose themselves' on the Tainos.

These people, the Tainos now realised, were the very Spanish who were restlessly coursing among their islands, searching for gold.

'Gold by Candlelight'

The Tainos in Cuba, like those in the rest of the Caribbean, wanted to get rid of these unwelcome visitors and so told them of another island, named Babeque, where, Columbus wrote down, 'people gather gold by candlelight at night in the sand and then with hammers make bars of it'. Who could believe such a childish tale? But Columbus, in his greed, did. Twice that November he attempted to set sail from Cuba to find Babeque, but each time storms drove him back. In the meantime, however, the lightest vessel, the *Pinta*, captained by Martin Pinzón, abandoned Columbus and took off on its own in search of the golden island 'because of greed'. (Pinzón eventually found Babeque, thought to be the modern island of Great Inagua, but there was no gold there.)

However, yet another rumour now wafted to Columbus' ears—the tale of a beautiful island called Bohio, which supposedly teemed with treasure. At the beginning of December 1492, the *Niña* and *Santa María* set sail across the strait now known as the Windward Passage and found themselves at an island of great beauty, which Columbus called *La Isla Española* because it reminded him so much of Spain with its evergreen and oak trees, broad plains, high mountains and even weather, which was 'wintry like October in Castile'. We now know the island as Hispaniola, the island divided into Haiti and the Dominican Republic.

Here, too, Columbus began to feel that at last he was much closer to the Indies and to treasures of gold. On 20 December, he anchored his two ships in Acul Bay, on Hispaniola's northern coast, a harbour so big that it could hold, Columbus assured his journal, 'all the ships in Christendom'. The local inhabitants were initially shy of encountering the Spanish, but then Columbus met the local *cacique*, one Guacanagari, and assured him that not only did the Spanish have the best of intentions, but that they would be happy to protect the locals from their enemies, the Caribs. He told Guacanagari that the Spanish would capture the Caribs, have them 'all brought with their hands bound' and would kill them. In order to demonstrate his power, Columbus then ordered a cannon and a musket fired, causing the Indians to fall to the ground in terror.

When they rose, however, they began to bring Columbus gifts, including an ornate belt whose buckle was a mask 'with two large ears, a tongue, and a nose of hammered gold'. Not only that, but Columbus had sent a scouting party along the coastline and they returned with the news that, in the interior of the island, there was a place, perhaps a mine, called Cibao (Columbus' ears once again heard Cipangu) where there was a vast store of gold. So, on 24 December, after feasting all night with the Tainos, Columbus set sail with his two vessels up the coastline. 'Our Lord in His mercy will direct me to find the gold mine', Columbus wrote. 'I have many people here who say they know where it is.'

By early Christmas Day, the two vessels were anchored off what is now Cape Hatien and Columbus decided to go to bed. ('I had not slept for two days and one night', he wrote, which gives one some indication of his exhausted and overheated state of mind.) No sooner did he fall asleep than he was awakened by a lookout's cries and a shudder that ran through the spine of the *Santa María*—it had run aground on a coral reef. Moving quickly, Columbus ordered the ship's owner, Juan de la Cosa, to lower a ship's boat, tie off to the stern of the *Santa María* and tow her off the reef. But La Cosa, in a panic, rowed instead to the nearby *Niña*, and the *Santa María*, forced against the reef by the waves, burst its seams and sank, although all hands aboard were saved.

Columbus, now on the *Niña*, tried to make the best of the fact that he was now down to only one ship (for Pinzón had still not returned with the *Pinta*). 'I recognised that our Lord has caused me to run aground at this place', he wrote, 'so that I might establish a settlement here'.

Villa de la Navidad

And so, in this most beautiful, fertile and gold-bearing of islands, Columbus built a fort, stripping the *Santa María*'s timbers to help do so. In honour of the Christmas sinking, it was called the Villa de la Navidad and he left forty men behind in order to man it—men who fought for the opportunity. They would trade for gold with the Tainos on the island; Guacanagari would organise the Indians' efforts, bringing the precious metal from the interior. It seemed like Providence had at last smiled on Christopher Columbus and he decided now to head for home. He had begun to suspect that the continued absence of Martin Pinzón meant that Pinzón had, in fact, begun to sail to Spain ahead of him, to claim all the glory as his own.

But before leaving his fort and men behind, Columbus decided that there should be one more demonstration of his power:

For this purpose, I ordered one lombard [cannon] loaded and fired at the side of the Santa María, which was aground. The King [Guacanagari] saw how far the lombard shot reached and how it passed through the side of the ship … I did all this so that the King would consider those I am leaving as friends, and also that he might fear them.

As Columbus sailed on 5 January, Martin Pinzón appeared on the *Pinta*. He told Columbus that he had, in fact, found Babeque, but that it had turned out to be devoid of gold, although he claimed to have found gold nuggets in exploring Hispaniola from the other side of the island. Columbus allowed Pinzón to join him on the return voyage. It was good to have two ships instead of one, but Columbus did not trust Pinzón, writing in his log: 'I do not know why he has been so disloyal and untrustworthy toward me. Even so, I am going to ignore these actions in order to prevent Satan from hindering this voyage, as he has done up until now'.

Even on his return voyage, Columbus chased down fables, stopping in northeastern Hispaniola to seek gold from Indians who may have been Caribs. They were armed with bows 'as large as those in France or England' and skirmished with the Spanish. After making one last side journey in search of an island populated only by women and visited seasonally by Carib warriors—naturally, he did not find it—Columbus sailed northeast in search of the southwesterly trades and then headed back to Spain. His journey back was as rough as his outward voyage had been easy—the *Niña* and *Pinta* were hit by two powerful storms that separated the ships—but at last Columbus found himself back in Spain, being honoured in front of the king and queen. He brought back with him green parrots, gold baubles—and Taino Indians, who gazed in wonder at what was, to them, a strange new world.

The Destruction of the Tainos

This was the high point of Christopher Columbus' life. He was to make three more voyages to the Americas and, despite increasing evidence to the contrary, never gave up believing that he had found the Indies. He was incensed at the Spanish government's refusal to give him ten per cent of the gold found in the New World, and died in 1506 at the age of fifty-five, an embittered man. In the meantime, the Spanish swarmed to the Caribbean and ultimately to Mexico and Peru, where the true golden treasures were found.

The Taino people who had initially met Columbus became slaves to the first wave of Spanish settlers to set up plantations in Cuba, Puerto Rico, Hispaniola and other places. The 'dressed people' had taken over the Taino paradise and set about the process of turning it into hell. The Tainos began to die off, either through starvation or through Old World diseases such as smallpox, for which they had no immunity. The Spanish also murdered them, by the hundreds of thousands. The Spanish friar Bartolomé de Las Casas estimated that three million Tainos had died by 1561. 'Who in future generations will believe this?' he asked plaintively.

Las Casas went on to describe the tortures the Indians were subjected to, from settlers who:

… made bets as to who would slit a man in two, or cut off his head at one blow; or they opened up his bowels. They tore the babes from their mother's breast by their feet, and dashed their heads against the rocks … they spitted the bodies of other babes, together with their mothers and all who were before them, on their swords … and by thirteens, in honour and reverence for our Redeemer and the twelve Apostles they put wood underneath and, with fire, they burned the Indians alive.

While some historians dispute the total numbers, the docile and naked people who met Columbus on Guanahaní, the island of welcome, would become nearly extinct by the beginning of the seventeenth century. It was just a small taste of what awaited the inhabitants of the New World over the next three centuries.

CHAPTER THREE

Encountering the World
Ferdinand Magellan circumnavigates the globe

Even in Magellan's time, they knew how important his voyage around the world had been. Writing only twenty years after the great sailor's death in the Philippines, the Spanish historian Gonzalo Fernandez de Oviedo effused: 'The track that [Magellan] followed is the most wonderful thing and the greatest novelty that has ever been seen since God created the first man and ordered the world unto our own day'.

Praise of this nature was not accorded even Columbus, and with good reason: Columbus sought the Indies—the Spice Islands—just as Magellan did, and merely blundered into the Americas. But Ferdinand Magellan, driven by passion, courage and anger, knew that the Pacific Ocean existed and knew that the Spice Islands lay on the other side of it. His dogged determination to find a way through ended up with him proving that a man could take a ship and sail around the planet Earth. As Oviedo further wrote: 'Nothing more notable in navigation [has] ever been heard or described since the voyage of the patriarch Noah'. And nothing more extraordinary would be done in terms of opening up human horizons until man landed on the moon.

Adventure and Betrayal

Ferdinand Magellan is hugely important in human history, yet we know relatively little about his early life. He was born, probably in 1480, in northern Portugal. His family were minor nobility fallen on hard times, although his father still had the connections to send twelve-year-old Ferdinand off to Lisbon, to serve as a page to the Portuguese Queen Leonor, wife of King John II. He seems to have received military training at court, not unusual for a young man of his relatively impoverished station—the other options would have been for him to become a colonial officer, a clerk or a priest—and began his life of adventure in 1505 when he sailed with a Portuguese expedition to India. He spent the next seven years fighting in the service of king and country as Portugal sought to colonise India, present-day Malaysia and the Moluccas—the Spice Islands themselves. These places were essential to Portugal if it were to compete for world hegemony against Spain, which had a stranglehold on the riches of the New World Columbus had discovered.

Magellan proved himself to be a courageous and loyal officer. He fought at Cochin, India, in 1510, participated in the attack on Goa the same year, and took part in the fall of Malacca, in modern Malaysia, in 1511. After briefly returning to Portugal, he again left for battle, fighting the Muslims in Morocco in 1512. It was here that he received a lance wound that partially severed the tendons at the back of his right knee and left him so lame that many people meeting him for the first time mistakenly thought he had a club foot. This injury changed Magellan's life in other ways, too. When he returned to Portugal, he asked for an annuity because of his injury, but he was turned down by King Manuel I, with the suggestion that his wound was not as disabling as he made it out to be. (In other versions of this story, Magellan was also accused of illegal trading with the Muslims in Morocco and refused further service by King Manuel, even though he was acquitted.)

Enraged by such treatment on the part of the country for which he had fought so long, Magellan turned his eyes to Spain.

Setting Off for the South Sea

Rage is often underrated as the mother of invention, and when Ferdinand Magellan arrived in Seville in October 1517 he had a plan to present to Charles V, King of Spain, Holy Roman Emperor and grandson of Ferdinand and Isabella. Magellan knew that Pope Leo X, acting as arbiter, had agreed that the eastern route to the Spice Islands—around the tip of Africa at the Cape of Good Hope—belonged to the Portuguese. If Spain, which, after all, was benefiting from the riches of the Americas, wanted to reach the Indies, then mariners would have to sail west to do so.

This was exactly what Magellan proposed to Charles—a way to compete with Portugal in its own backyard. The ocean called the 'South Sea' had been discovered when Vasco Nùñez de Balboa crossed Panama, and it was Magellan's notion that he could find a western route to it. Along with his friend, the astronomer Rui Faleiro, Magellan poured over maps and charts of the Americas. He knew that the continent had been explored by John Cabot to the north and that Amerigo Vespucci had charted it as far south as Brazil. Magellan was certain, he told the king, that with the right backing he could travel even farther south and find a way to the South Sea.

King Charles was bright and ambitious, although only eighteen years old, and he saw the merit in Magellan's scheme. He thus had a contract drawn up agreeing to provide the Portuguese navigator (although by this time Magellan had assumed Spanish citizenship) with a fleet of five ships, along with the money to hire five crews. Magellan was awarded the military title 'captain-general' and would become governor of any islands he discovered. In return, the king would receive four-fifths of the proceeds of the voyage.

Magellan was ecstatic, even though more pitfalls lay ahead. The ships—his flagship, the *Trinidad*, the *Victoria*, the *Concepción*, the *San Antonio* and the *Santiago*—were old, small and poorly armed, a fact remarked upon by a spy for King Manuel of Portugal, who was keeping a jealous eye on Magellan's doings: 'I assure your Highness that I should be ill-inclined to sail in them [even] for the Canaries'.

Also, Magellan was forced to sail with three Spanish captains in his fleet, because the Spanish were worried that too many Portuguese were on the expedition. But, finally, all was in readiness. Accompanied by his slave Enrique, who would prove invaluable as an interpreter, Magellan boarded the *Trinidad* and his little fleet set sail on 20 September 1519.

'The Great and Awful Things'

Along with his 250 officers, crew and soldiers, Magellan had along with him a passenger, one Antonio Pigafetta of Venice. Pigafetta was probably in his late twenties, a man of noble birth and some means. There is some mystery as to what he was doing with Magellan. Some sources indicate that he was the kind of adventuring gentleman who would become familiar on journeys of exploration in later centuries—a tourist out for extreme thrills. But there has also been the suggestion that he was a spy for Venice, the city-state most hurt by the Portuguese—and now, potentially, Spanish—inroads into the lucrative eastern spice trade. Whatever his motives, Pigafetta would provide the only complete record we have of Magellan's epic journey—of 'the very great and awful things of the Ocean', as he put it—and he also came, during the course of the trip, to admire the captain-general immensely.

The first part of the trip was familiar. Magellan set sail south for the Canary Islands and Cape Verde, and then headed west across the Atlantic, from the bulge of Africa to the bulge of Brazil. But the trip from its very beginning was not without incident. The weather was troublesome. At first, the vessels were often becalmed, at which point they were, according to Pigafetta, surrounded 'by great fish called *tiburoni* [sharks] … which have terrible teeth and eat men when they find them alive or dead in the sea'. Then storms arose that were so violent the tops of the masts tipped to touch the tops of the waves and lightning was so fierce that St Elmo's fire—static electricity that often gathers at mast-tops during storms—was seen for hours in the rigging.

But the weather was not the most serious problem: that was Magellan's relationship with the Spanish captains and crew members. Magellan was a hard taskmaster and insisted that his fleet follow him closely and take no actions without his approval. Even at night, they had to watch the rear of the *Trinidad* for a series of torches that would give them direction—one torch to change tack, two to reduce speed and so on. The proud Spanish captains of three of the ships thought their competency was being called into question. One of them, Captain Juan de Cartagena of the *San Antonio*, refused a direct order from Magellan, causing Magellan to relieve him of his command and put him in irons.

By the time the fleet reached Brazil, after a crossing of seventy days, discontent ran rampant through the expedition.

Painting with Fire

Because of Pigafetta's journal, we have an unusually detailed picture of Magellan's encounter with the inhabitants of Brazil—it was known as 'the land of Verzin', after *verzino*, the Italian name for the brazil wood trees that grew there in abundance. Pigafetta wrote, correctly, that the country is 'very vast and larger than Spain, Portugal, France and Italy combined'. He was not quite so accurate about other things. The people who thronged in dugout canoes to meet Magellan's ships reach an age of '125 to 140 years', the Italian gentleman wrote, mainly because they live their lives 'according to the laws of nature', even though they are also cannibals. But Pigafetta did note that the people slept in great longhouses and 'paint their whole body and the face in a wonderful manner with fire', meaning tattoos. He also sniffed that the Indians 'dress up in parrot feathers with a huge wheel [of feathers] on their backsides, in such a fashion that it looks ridiculous'.

Magellan and his fleet sailed 3000 kilometres (2000 miles) down the Brazilian coastline and spent some time refitting in the protected harbour of present-day Rio de Janeiro. There, Pigafetta and the other crew members traded with the Brazilian tribes quite satisfactorily: 'For a king of playing cards', wrote the Italian traveller, 'the Indians gave me five fowles, and even thought they cheated me'. Soon enough, however, Magellan pushed the fleet farther south, looking for a passageway that would lead west. By January 1520 they had reached latitude 35 degrees south, farther than any European had gone. Still they continued in search of a western passageway, even as the weather turned colder. South of today's Montevideo, the fleet met its first penguins. Pigafetta reported that they were present in such numbers that 'in one hour they were able to fill their five ships with geese [penguins], and they are completely black and unable to fly and they live on fish, and are so fat it is necessary to peel them'.

Winter—and Mutiny

By this time March was ending and the southern winter was about to begin. Magellan took his fleet to a small harbour at a place he called Port St Julian, in what is now southern Argentina. He gathered the crew together and told them that they would winter there for five months and that they would have to exist on half-rations during that time. This enraged many of the men, especially the Spanish captains, who on the night of 1 April staged a violent mutiny. They took over the *San Antonio* and killed its captain, a Portuguese man who was a friend of Magellan's, and then put Juan de Cartagena (clapped in irons previously by Magellan) in charge of the vessel. When Magellan awoke, he found he was in command only of the *Trinidad* and the *Santiago*, which was captained by João Serráo, a friend of his brother.

Magellan, with typical stubborn courage and audacity, fought back. He sent five crewmen in a longboat with a letter to one of the rebellious captains, agreeing to a parlay. As the man opened the missive, one of Magellan's crewmen stabbed him to death. Sailors loyal to Magellan quickly captured the other ships. The ringleader of the mutineers was executed and his body drawn and quartered, while Cartagena was marooned on this wild and remote shore when the fleet finally set sail in the spring. He was never seen again.

Magellan sentenced forty other mutineers to death but then pardoned them, earning their gratitude, although there still remained malcontents. As winter wore on, Magellan explored this wide, flat, freezing area, which he named Patagonia because the Telhuelche Indians who lived there had such big feet and wore huge shoes made out of thick skin and stuffed with straw (*patagon* in Portuguese means a huge, clumsy foot). In fact, these Indians fascinated Pigafetta and the rest of the Europeans. In their first encounter with one, they saw 'a man as large as a giant … dancing and singing and putting dust on his head'. Magellan ordered that the man be brought to him and when he came near, the Patagonian 'was struck with great wonder, and he made a sign with his upraised finger, believing that [the Europeans] came from the sky'. This giant was supposedly so tall that the Europeans did not even reach his waist. According to Pigafetta, this altogether extraordinary figure had 'a large face, encircled with yellow paint and two hearts painted on his two cheeks, [and] his hair dyed white'.

The Europeans were fascinated by Patagonian customs—'when these people feel sick to their stomachs', Pigafetta wrote, and one can hear the Italian gentleman grimace, 'they thrust an arrow into their throats to the depth of two palms and more and vomit up a green-coloured substance mixed with blood'. Not contenting themselves with staring, the sailors tried to capture a few of these giants and ultimately trapped two, 'who began to blow and foam at the mouth like bulls'. Cramped in the hold of one of the ships, both men were to die within the year. As a last adventure of this terrible winter, Magellan sent his friend João Serrão, commanding the *Santiago*, southward, but a storm wrecked the ship 100 kilometres (70 miles) away. Serrão and all his crew but one made it safely to shore, but his trek back to Magellan's camp is one of the unsung epics of endurance in history.

The Pacific Sea

On 18 October, in the southern spring, Magellan set sail south with his fleet, now reduced to four ships. Within three days' sailing time, they came upon a cape that Magellan named the Cape of Eleven Thousand Virgins. Beyond the cape was an inlet and at the end of the inlet there was what Pigafetta called 'a very hidden strait', extremely narrow, with high mountains on either side of it. The fleet anchored there, finding that the water was so deep that their anchors would not reach the bottom and they were forced to tie up to the land. The next morning, Magellan told his captains that he had seen this strait marked on a secret map in the archives of the King of Portugal and that this strait led to the Southern Ocean. Although this was a lie, even Pigafetta reported it as the truth. It gave Magellan's officers the courage to proceed down this narrow, windy corridor, with mountains looming over it, that everyone but Magellan assumed was a river.

The *Concepción* and the *San Antonio* went ahead to reconnoitre. They were gone for so long that Magellan and the others aboard the *Trinidad* and *Victoria* thought them lost, but suddenly they heard a great commotion of guns—the two vessels had returned and were firing off signal cannon.

It turned out the strait had opened up into a bay, and then proceeded into a larger bay, at which point the two ships had returned to report to Magellan that, just possibly, there was a way through here. All four vessels now proceeded, with Magellan leading the way, carefully moving between islands, through narrow channels, taking soundings in order to avoid running aground. They came to a point where the channel divided, with one strait leading to the southwest, while another turned southeast. Magellan took the southwest route with the *Trinidad* and *Victoria*, leaving the *San Antonio* and the *Concepción* to explore the southeast. After sailing for a short time, Magellan anchored and sent a ship's boat ahead to explore. The boat was gone for three days and came back with the momentous news that they had found 'a great and wide sea'.

Magellan was so moved that he wept. But then came bad news: the *Concepción* returned from its search to the southeast, but the *San Antonio*—the expedition's largest and most well-supplied vessel—did not. After searching fruitlessly for the ship, it became apparent that it had probably turned around and headed back to Spain, deserting Magellan (as, in fact, was the case).

But Magellan would not be stopped. 'On Wednesday the twenty-eighth of November, 1520', wrote Pigafetta proudly, 'we issued forth from the said strait and entered the Pacific Sea'.

A Mouse for a Ducat

The ocean they entered had heretofore been called the South Sea, but Magellan was so impressed with its long, calm, rolling swells that he renamed it the Pacific. The first thing he did was turn his vessels northward and sail up the west coast of South America, always keeping land in sight in the far distance. According to a pilot on the *Trinidad*, they kept their northern course for twenty-three straight days. Pigafetta wondered at the sights of the ocean, particularly the flying fish, called *colondrins*, from the Spanish word for a swallow. When predatory albacores or bonitos encountered the *colondrins*, Pigafetta wrote, 'the flying fish immediately leap out of the water and fly as far as a bowshot without wetting their wings. But the other fish dart under the shadows of the flying fish, and no sooner do they fall into the water, than they are immediately seized and eaten'.

By 22 December, the fleet had made 2500 kilometres (1600 miles) up the coast of South America and was now opposite Chile. With the climate warming and the sailing easy, Magellan turned due west and now headed straight out into the Pacific, coursing over uncharted waters. He had, however, made a serious mistake. Drastically underestimating the size of the Pacific—he thought it was 3000 kilometres (2000 miles) across, rather than 20,000 kilometres (13,000 miles)—he had not stopped at any harbour along the coast of South America to find fresh water and food. At first, this mistake was not apparent and the men on Magellan's ships found their swift passage exhilarating. 'We made each day fifty or sixty leagues or more', wrote Pigafetta, borne along by a strong wind and by a current, the South Equatorial Drift, which coursed due west. But all became alarmed when they had travelled for 5000 kilometres (3000 miles) without sighting any land at all, let alone the Spice Islands.

By mid-January, the crews were suffering terribly. Pigafetta records the misery:

They ate biscuits, and when there were no more [biscuits], they ate the crumbs, which were full of maggots and smelled strongly of mouse urine. They drank yellow water, already several days putrid … A mouse would bring half a ducat or a ducat. The gums of some of the men swelled over their upper and lower teeth, so that they could not eat, and so died. And nineteen men died from their sickness …

The Island of Thieves

Magellan's error in not reprovisioning his ships was compounded by his bad luck. Had he continued sailing west, he would have come to Tahiti, a land of plenty. But instead, faced with the suffering of his crew, he turned to the northwest, heading more directly to the Equator, since he knew the Spice Islands lay along that latitude. He was still far from the Moluccas but, even so, would have found his way to the Marquesas Islands had his crew not spotted a huge, stacked cumulus cloud, a sign of land, and steered again southwest, only to find the tiny island of Pukapuka, where swift currents and deep water kept the fleet from landing.

Sailing on, with men dying daily, Magellan finally made landfall at another island, which was probably Caroline Island, a place where the harbour swarmed with sharks, which the hungry men fished for, despite risking loss of life or limb to one of the snapping *tiburoni*. At last, on 6 March, with many of the men now too weak to handle the sails, Magellan came upon two islands belonging to the Marianas chain. He anchored near the biggest one, probably Guam, hoping to rest his crew and bring fresh supplies aboard. But his encounter with the tribes of Guam was a startling and violent one. Immediately after the little fleet anchored, the islanders—whose lack of experience with Europeans did not make them the slightest bit shy—swarmed all over Magellan's ships, stealing whatever was not tied down, 'to such an extent that our men could not protect their belongings', Pigafetta wrote. Magellan, normally even-handed, lost his temper when the islanders, in their fast-moving skiffs with triangular sails, stole one of the ship's boats tied directly under the poop deck of the *Trinidad*. He sent ashore a force of forty armed men, who killed at least seven of the islanders with crossbows. Having no experience with European weapons, the reaction of the wounded natives was startling. Pigafetta wrote that 'whenever we wounded any of these people with a shaft that entered their body, they looked at it and then marvellously drew it out, and so died forthwith'.

Having set fire to forty huts, the shore party made their way back to the ships. So hungry were the weakened men on board, according to Pigafetta, that they begged the landing party for the entrails of those they had killed, so that they might have fresh meat.

'Rational people'

Leaving this horrific scene behind, Magellan sailed on for another week before sighting Samar, an island in the Philippines. At first, it seemed as if they had arrived in paradise. Resting on the beach near two fresh streams—the water tasting as fine as the finest wine to men who had been drinking ship's water from which they had had to strain the algae with their teeth—and eating fresh fruit and coconuts, the crew began to recover. Magellan himself, according to Pigafetta, walked among the men giving them coconut milk to drink.

Samar was uninhabited, but within a few days of their landing, the Europeans were visited by a delegation of islanders from a nearby island. Much to the relief of Magellan and his crew, these were 'rational people', unlike the thieves on Guam. After Magellan gave them gifts of mirrors, combs and bells, they returned the favour with fish, palm wine and figs. They left, but promised to return in four days with more food, and this they did, coming back laden with supplies for the hungry men, and this time bringing their chief and other dignitaries. These men wore gold jewellery, but Magellan, unlike Columbus and his men, did not press them for its source. Instead, proceeding with great diplomacy, he insisted on exchanging gifts and treating those he met as equals. His slave Enrique, originally Malaysian, understood the Tagalog language of the islanders and helped translate.

After eight days of rest, Magellan now sailed his ships farther into the Surigao Strait, exploring the islands. On 28 March, Holy Thursday, Magellan anchored off the island of Limasawa and decided to observe Easter there. He put on a glorious show, celebrating a Mass, shooting off cannon (which, as usual, overawed the watching islanders) and having his men display their fencing ability. After this, he erected a cross, telling the islanders that any Spanish ships that happened by in the future would see this sign and would therefore leave them in peace, except to trade with them.

'Our Mirror, Our Light, Our Comfort'

For the next month, Magellan and his three ships coursed through the Philippines, with Magellan making contact with the island peoples and their 'rajahs', or chiefs. With his fine but at times prurient eye for detail, Pigafetta continued to observe the people they encountered. They all went about naked, except 'for a bit of cloth over their shameful parts'. The men 'have their members pierced from one side to the other, with a golden spike as thick as a goose quill … Some have a pointed star above the glands of the member, also of gold'.

Unfortunately, this idyll would soon end. Near the end of April, arriving at the island of Cebu, Magellan befriended a chief named Zula, who begged Magellan to do battle against his rival on a nearby island, a rajah named Lapulapu. Here Magellan had trapped himself, for his displays of Spanish power—the cannon, the swords, the armour—would be seen as mere braggadocio if he would not help those who had become his allies.

So, on the morning of 27 April, Magellan anchored off the island of Mactan, Lapulapu's home. Perhaps 1500 angry islanders could be seen milling about on the shore, carrying wooden spears whose tips had been sharpened and hardened in fire. Because the water was extremely shallow for up to 800 metres (2600 feet) offshore, Magellan's three ships were unable to approach the beach and, therefore, their cannon—the outnumbered Europeans' trump card—would be useless in the fight.

Undaunted, Magellan put on his armour and prepared to lead a party of some sixty men to the shore. Pigafetta and others implored him not to join the soldiers—Pigafetta relates, 'we begged him not to go there, but like a good captain, he did not want to abandon his allies'. Magellan and his men, Pigafetta with them, were forced to wade for hundreds of metres to the beach in full armour. When they got close to shore, they were assailed by islanders throwing wooden lances, shooting darts from blowpipes and throwing rocks and chunks of coral. The situation quickly deteriorated. Magellan sent a squad to burn the huts of the islanders, thinking this might intimidate them, as it had the people of Guam, but it merely enraged the warriors further, and they pressed in on the Europeans from all sides. Magellan ordered his men to withdraw slowly, but instead they took panic and fled back through the shallows, leaving Magellan to fight on accompanied by Pigafetta and only six or eight others.

The enemy, Pigafetta wrote, 'recognised the Captain [Magellan] and so many assailed him that twice they knocked the sallet [helmet] off his head. And he, like a good knight, continued to stand firm with a few others and for more than an hour refused to retreat'. But then the end came swiftly: 'An Indian threw his bamboo spear into [Magellan's] face and he immediately killed him with his own spear, but it remained in [the Indian's] body'. Magellan tried to draw his sword, but a wound in his right arm made this difficult. Seeing this, one of the islanders 'with a large javelin thrust it into [Magellan's] left leg, whereby he fell face downward. On this, all at once rushed upon him … and slew our mirror, our light, our comfort and our true guide'.

A Miraculous Circumnavigation

In shock, Pigafetta and the surviving Europeans fought their way back to the ships. They sought to parlay with the Mactan islanders to get Magellan's body back, but they refused, saying that 'they wanted to keep him so that they would not forget him', a tribute to Magellan's courage. There was nothing to do but keep sailing, but the journey back to Spain would be a long, arduous and treacherous one. Soon after Magellan died, his slave Enrique asked for his freedom, claiming that Magellan had promised this to him. He was denied by Duarte Barbosa, one of the new captains—the other was João Serrão—and, therefore, slipped ashore at one island and plotted with the islanders against the Spanish. One night at a feast, the Spanish were attacked and many were massacred, including Serráo.

After wandering for a month through the Philippines, the decision was made to scuttle the *Concepción*, since there were no longer enough men to crew it—there were now only 130 left out of the 250 who had originally left Spain. Everyone was transferred to the *Trinidad* and the *Victoria* and the ships set sail for the Spice Islands, finally arriving at these much-dreamed-of isles in December. Wary of the Portuguese, the two ships quickly loaded up with cargoes of cloves and set sail on 18 December, but the *Trinidad* began taking on water and was forced to turn back to harbour for repairs, and thence to set forth on its own incredible odyssey. The *Victoria* steered past Timor and out into the Indian Ocean, from whence it rounded the Cape of Good Hope, reaching the South Atlantic on 19 May 1522. But, faced with rough weather, their journey was so slow that more and more men began to die of starvation and scurvy.

'We sailed northwest for two months,' Pigafetta wrote, 'and in that short space of time twenty-one men died'. With his eye for the curious and macabre, Pigafetta also noted that 'when they throw the Christian bodies into the sea, they sink to the bottom face up, and the Indians [Moluccans who had been hired at the Spice Islands to help crew the vessel] sink face down'.

Desperately, the *Victoria* put in at the Portuguese-held Cape Verde Islands to find food, but the Portuguese captured three men who had been sent ashore to bargain, and so the rest set sail immediately. Finally, on Sunday, 8 September 1522, the *Victoria* dropped anchor in the port of Seville, Spain. The ship's guns blasted out. Eighteen men out of Magellan's original 250 had arrived back. Starving, they tottered off the ship and 'gave thanks to God, in our shirts, barefooted, and with torches in our hands'.

Magellan had not made the entire journey, but without him none of these men would have either. And his opening up of the Pacific—and its peoples— to European influence would forever alter the course of history. Although Spain would never profit from the spice trade the way the Portuguese would, the Philippines, already indelibly marked by Magellan's presence, would become a rich possession for the Spanish crown for nearly four hundred years.

CHAPTER FOUR

The Great Walk
Cabeza de Vaca encounters America

In December of 1537, a small, grim-faced man could be seen haunting the court of King Charles V in Valladolid, Spain. Nearly fifty years old, he wore the fine clothing of a gallant soldier and royal appointee, which in fact he had been, but those who encountered him found his presence disturbing. The man seemed uncomfortable not just in his clothes, but in his very skin. He was extremely restless and hard to engage in conversation, yet sometimes he would not stop talking. He could be seen staring off into space or muttering to himself. He did not suffer those he considered to be fools patiently or gladly. *He*, however, had an important tale to tell, and he needed to tell it to King Charles himself.

The man's name was Álvar Núñez Cabeza de Vaca and that December he would get his chance to talk to the king. For despite his surly and off-putting manner, he had experienced something no other Spaniard—or other European, for that matter—had experienced. Along with two other white men and one black slave, he had walked 4000 kilometres (2500 miles) across the unknown area the Spanish knew only as *La Florida*—the vast lands north and east of Mexico. In doing so, as the historian Andres Resendez writes, Cabeza de Vaca and his friends instituted 'an extraordinary instance of first contacts between peoples whose ancestors had remained apart for 12,000 years'.

This was not the type of contact that Hernán Cortés, Francisco Pizarro or Hernando de Soto fostered, marked by plundering and killing, but contact of an entirely different sort. For Cabeza de Vaca lived among the Indians he met in a number of guises—as supplicant, slave, trader, and finally healer and shaman. And he knew them not as people to be robbed of their treasures, or as chattels, but as human beings.

From our view, half a millennium later, Cabeza de Vaca's story is one of the few glimpses we have into cultures that were about to be lost forever. This is what makes his journey and the narrative he later wrote of it (his *Relación*) so valuable, even if, ultimately, King Charles V did not think so.

The Young Soldier

Álvar Núñez Cabeza de Vaca had a name that made some of his contemporaries snicker, since Cabeza de Vaca literally meant 'head of a cow'. But those who laughed were not aware of his illustrious forebears. He was born in the province of Andalusia, in a town called Jerez de la Frontera, about 80 kilometres (50 miles) south of Seville—a place famous for the sweet wine the English called 'sherry'. Cabeza de Vaca's unusual name comes from a probably apocryphal tale: that a humble shepherd ancestor of Cabeza de Vaca's mother placed a cow's head at a mountain pass, thus guiding King Alfonso VIII of Castile to victory over the Moors at the battle of Las Navas de Tolosa in 1212. But Cabeza de Vaca did have a distinguished lineage. His grandfather, Pedro de Vera Mendoza, was one of the conquerors of the Canary Islands. Another relative was the famous musician Luis Cabeza de Vaca, who was a tutor to King Charles I (who later became Holy Roman Emperor and thus Charles V). Luis was probably the one who introduced the young Cabeza de Vaca to the Spanish court.

Despite these illustrious family members, Cabeza de Vaca had a difficult upbringing. Both his parents died while he was still a teenager and, with no inheritance, he turned to soldiering to make his way in life. He fought with gallantry with the Spanish forces in Italy from 1511 to 1513 and thereafter won favour with King Charles by helping put down a rebellion against the Spanish crown around 1520. By now, Cabeza de Vaca—short of stature, but highly ambitious—had married and needed more in life than the uncertain spoils of a soldier. In 1527, through his connections at the Spanish court, he was appointed Royal Treasurer—essentially, second-in-command—of an expedition that was about to plunge into the unknown wilderness of the New World known as *La Florida*.

'On Your Royal Conscience'

La Florida was essentially the entire Gulf Coast of America from Mexico—known as New Spain—to the current state of Florida. In the 1520s very few Europeans had visited this area. One of them was Ponce de León from Spain who had sought the so-called 'Fountain of Youth' in a legendary land called Bimini, which supposedly existed north of the Bahamas. Ponce de León landed on the Atlantic coast of what is now Florida during Easter week—the so-called 'Flowery Festival' or *Pascua Florida*, which is how the area got its name.

Hernán Cortés had conquered Mexico in 1519–20 and found riches beyond belief there, and many Spaniards were certain that north of Mexico there would be another civilisation filled with gold and silver. There were any number of ambitious Spanish explorers ready to investigate these lands, but few had any idea of what they were dealing with. All underestimated New World distances. Such vast expanses simply did not exist within the old, European world. Therefore, it was thought that the distance from the River of Palms (*Rio de las Palmas*) in eastern Mexico to Florida was only a matter of a few hundred kilometres. Instead, it was 4,000 kilometres (2500 miles).

The one-eyed conquistador Pánfilo de Narváez, who headed the expedition that Cabeza de Vaca joined, certainly believed this. Narváez is not one of history's most sympathetic figures. Cabeza de Vaca's exact contemporary, he had taken part in the conquest of Jamaica in 1509 and in 1520 was sent by Governor Diego Velázquez to halt the conquest of the Mexica by Cortés—Velázquez had decided Cortés was taking too much of this rich pie for himself. As a reward for his efforts, Narváez lost an eye to the pike of one of Cortés' men and was imprisoned by Cortés in Mexico for three years.

Once he was allowed to return to Spain, he begged King Charles for an expedition of his own, claiming that he was seeking the conversion of the Indians. He did not, he said, want it to 'weigh heavily on your royal conscience' if these poor pagans were not brought to the light of Christ. Of course, other considerations came into play, mainly the riches that might be gained by such an expedition, and in the end Charles allowed Narváez a huge land grant. He gave Cortés the southern half of Mexico, but bestowed all else north of the River of Palms and east to Florida on Narváez. By being successful in such an expedition, Narváez could outshine his old rival Cortés, as well as greatly increase the riches and lands of the kingdom of Spain.

It is doubtful that Narváez chose Cabeza de Vaca as his Royal Treasurer, since it was understood that a patent from the king included numerous royal appointees. Three other men who joined Narváez and who would help make history with Cabeza de Vaca were captains Alonso del Castillo and Andrés Dorantes, as well as Dorantes' North African slave, Estabancio.

'A Colossal Navigation Mistake'

Narváez's fleet of five ships left Spain on 17 June 1527 with six hundred men. They arrived in Cuba in the early autumn, but a hurricane then devastated the fleet to such an extent that Narváez was forced to delay sailing from Cuba until April 1528. Finally, his ships set sail for *La Florida*. Here there occurred what one historian has called 'a colossal error in navigation' on the part of Narváez's navigator, Diego Miruelo. The actual destination of the expedition was the River of Palms, in northeastern Mexico (probably today's Rio Soto la Marina) on the *western* side of the Gulf of Mexico. But fighting contrary gales, their progress slowed by the Gulf Stream, which here runs from northwest to southeast, the little fleet was guided by Miruelo to the west coast of the Florida Peninsula, on the *eastern* side of the Gulf, an error of some 1500 kilometres (930 miles). The fleet landed, probably in the vicinity of modern-day Sarasota, in Tampa Bay, on Easter Sunday.

It is hard to understand, even with the rather primitive dead reckoning navigation of the day, how such a mistake could have been made, but when Narváez first set foot on the Florida coast and claimed it for Spain, he thought he was actually in northern Mexico, just a few hundred kilometres south of the River of Palms. All the disasters of the expedition followed from this one crucial mistake.

The first contact the Spanish had with the local Indians was uneasy. The first tribe they met made 'signs and threatening gestures' at the Spanish, as Cabeza de Vaca wrote in his *Relación*, but retreated when Narváez ordered the passengers aboard the ships to disembark. This horde of people—and horses, which the local Indians would not have seen before—frightened the Indians enough to make some flee, while the others agreed to trade with the Spanish. But, moving a little farther inland, a Spanish scouting expedition found a tribe in the possession of 'many crates belonging to Castilian merchants, and in each one of them was the body of a dead man, and the bodies were covered with painted deer hides'.

Along with the crates the Spanish found numerous Spanish items, such as shoes and pieces of iron. It was obvious a ship had been wrecked along this coast, probably a vessel heading east from Mexico, and that the Indians had treated the remains of the survivors almost worshipfully. But the priests who were along on the Spanish expedition thought that the way in which the bodies had been preserved smacked of 'idolatry' and so ordered them, and the crates, to be burned, much to the displeasure of the Indians. When the Spanish then asked the Indians, who possessed a few pieces of gold, where they could get more of the precious metal, the Indians were only too happy to point them northward, claiming there was another tribe, 'in a province called Apalachee', who owned all the treasure the Spanish could hope for.

The Bay of Horses

Narváez now called a conference of his captains, who included Cabeza de Vaca, as well as Alonso del Castillo and Andrés Dorantes. He told them that Miruelo had assured him that the River of Palms was only a few hundred kilometres distant, to the north, and that therefore he had decided to split up his force. His ships would sail up the coast with his sailors and settlers, while the military contingent of the expedition, some three hundred men strong, would go overland, keeping to the coast, to discover this gold-laden land of the Apalachee. Cabeza de Vaca protested greatly against this decision, telling Narváez 'by no means should he leave the ships as [the pilots] ... did not know where they were' and that the army would be 'travelling mute, that is, without interpreters [through] a land about which we had no information'. At least, he says he did—there were no survivors to contradict him when he finally put his story down in writing in his *Relación* in 1542. But there is a record of others protesting—a woman who was along on the expedition gave a dire warning to Narváez that, in the end, went unheeded. He was the leader of the *adelantamiento* and his word would be obeyed.

It was the second fateful—and fatal—error of the expedition. Narváez's ships sailed off, planning to rendezvous with him farther up the coast, while Narváez led his men overland. Perhaps something might still have been salvaged from the expedition had he actually kept to the coastline, but he turned his men much farther inland and they soon found themselves struggling through the Florida swamps with little to eat, sweltering in the heat. Cabeza de Vaca, Castillo and Dorantes begged Narváez to turn back to the coast or at least to send scouts westward to establish contact with the ships but, intent on the imagined trail of the Apalachee, Narváez refused. For over a month they wandered, capturing Indians to use as guides. They finally came to the land of the Apalachee, where they battled the Indians, only to find a poor, threadbare land, with no gold or other precious metals. Not only that, but the Indians were natural guerrilla fighters, shooting arrows with deadly accuracy from their long bows, killing any conquistador who ventured out alone, before melting away into the woods.

For three months, the Spanish marched and countermarched through the countryside, seeking larger and more prosperous Apalachee villages (these did exist, but much farther north). Fifty men died, of Indian arrows, starvation and disease. Finally, Narváez could take it no more and decided that they had to make their way back to the sea. Arriving near the coast, they found themselves in a land of shallow estuaries, near a muddy bay that was only waist deep. There were no ships in sight. (In fact, the mariners of the fleet, pushed farther out to sea by shallow water and unable to find the River of Palms, had finally realised their error in assuming Florida was Mexico. After searching fruitlessly for Narváez and his men, they returned to Cuba.)

When Narváez realised that help was not forthcoming, he decided that he and his men needed to save themselves. Stranded in what they called the Bay of Horses, because they had to kill a horse every third day just to stay alive, the starving conquistadors desperately built five rafts from pine or cypress trees, caulking them with resin and tying them together with sinews from the legs of their horses. They stitched together sails made from deer skins. Each raft was about 10 metres (22 feet) long and rode only about 20 centimetres (8 inches) above the water when fully loaded with fifty men and supplies. Yet, 'so greatly can necessity prevail', wrote Cabeza de Vaca, 'that it made us risk going in this manner and placing ourselves in a sea so treacherous, and without any one of us … having any knowledge of the art of navigation'.

The rafts pushed off on 22 September 1528.

'Like Giants'

Keeping as close to the coastline as possible, the five rafts sailed for about a month along the Gulf of Mexico. In their weakened state, the Spanish tried to avoid landing, but soon they began to run out of water, since the water bags they had fashioned out of the hollowed legs of horses had begun to rot. Men dehydrated quickly in the hot sun. Some began to drink seawater and died. Finally, the rafts encountered canoes with Indians, who guided them to shore and fed them, but then turned on them in the night, attacking and killing several men.

The Spaniards managed to set the rafts afloat again and escape, but as they journeyed westward they were again attacked by hostile Indians when they tried to land. At last they reached the broad mouth of the Mississippi River, whose powerful current sent fresh water kilometres out to sea so the Spanish were able to slake their thirsts. But no sooner had they relaxed than a powerful storm arose, separating the rafts. After several days, Cabeza de Vaca spotted another raft on the horizon and ordered his men to row for it. This raft turned out to be Narváez's, which was sailing far more strongly than Cabeza de Vaca's own vessel. Cabeza de Vaca begged Narváez to throw him a line and tow him toward shore, but Narváez refused, claiming he had now relinquished command of the expedition and that it was every man for himself.

Narváez then sailed off, leaving Cabeza de Vaca and his men to fend for themselves. Narváez's fate and that of most of the other conquistadors was to be a dire one, but after a day more at sea, with his companions near death, Cabeza de Vaca heard the sound of surf breaking and saw land about 5 kilometres (3 miles) away. The men who could still move frantically rowed for land and the raft was finally tossed upon the beach by a large wave. The men left the raft 'half-walking, half-crawling'. Huddled under a sandy bluff, they drank rainwater, built a fire and roasted some cornmeal they had with them. Cabeza de Vaca sent out one man, Lope de Oviedo, to climb a nearby tree and take their bearings. He came back with the news that they were on a long and narrow island. (Scholars have long debated just which island this is, but most now agree that it was an island off the coast of the present-day state of Texas, just south of Galveston Island.) He claimed that 'the land was rutted in a way that it usually is when cattle roam', which meant to the Spanish that Christians inhabited the island.

This hope was dashed when Oviedo ventured forth again and found himself being followed by three Indians with bows and arrows. Very soon, the castaways were surrounded by a hundred Indians, all with bows and arrows. 'Whether or not they were of great stature', Cabeza de Vaca later wrote, 'our fear made them seem like giants'.

Tossed ashore, away from all that was, to them, civilisation, without arms, armour or horses, Cabeza de Vaca and his companions were at last meeting, face to face, the inhabitants of the North American continent. It was 6 November 1528.

The Slaves

The Indians that the Spanish met were either from the Han or Capoques tribe, both of which used the island as their winter habitation. At first, they displayed extraordinary generosity to Cabeza de Vaca and his fellows, bringing them food in the form of roots and fish. Still, their presence made the Spanish nervous (the Indians were, in fact, over 1.8 metres (6 feet) tall, with powerful physiques) and they made an attempt to sail off the island, taking off their clothes as they pushed the raft into the water. Unfortunately, the raft capsized, with the loss of two men, and the Spanish, now naked, were cast ashore. When the Indians returned the next day and saw them in such a miserable state, they began weeping at their plight. Novembers in the region are frigid and were even more so at a time when the climate was cooler than it is today; they knew the Spanish were going to be in trouble.

The Indians literally carried the white men to large fires they had made and allowed them to warm themselves. Although at first Cabeza de Vaca and his men did not realise it, the raft that carried Andrés Dorantes and Alonso del Castillo, which Cabeza de Vaca had not seen since the storm arose near the mouth of the Mississippi, had landed on the opposite side of the island and the men aboard it also found themselves being cared for by Indians. But in a short time this situation changed. The winter of 1528–29 was to be one of the harshest the region had ever experienced, food was scarce, and the Han or Capoques (for it is not clear which tribe took in which group of Spaniards) could not be expected to feed these strangers forever, particularly when their own diets consisted of little more than roots and what fish they could catch.

Of the eighty Spaniards in the two groups that had arrived on the island—which they began to call *Malhado*, or the Island of Doom—only fifteen survived as spring came on. And those who did survive had become slaves. This did not happen in the organised way that Europeans enslaved people but came about little by little. Certain Spaniards, afraid of becoming victims of the type of human sacrifice that existed among the Mexica (but not these tribes), chose to live by themselves on the beach but were eventually so desperate with hunger that they began to eat their dead. This horrified the Indians, who never practised cannibalism, and it seems to have dehumanised the Europeans in their eyes. The Indians also caught a disease, probably dysentery, from the Spanish. And probably half of the 400 or so Indians died. In their great rage, the survivors nearly killed the remaining Spaniards, but instead decided to enslave them.

Escape from Malhado

Cabeza de Vaca's slavery was harsh. The Han or Capoques forced him to carry heavy loads and to wander completely naked through swamps digging for roots. The slightest offence would earn him a slap across the face or a beating with a stick. The Indians could be as harsh as they had been generous, killing three Spanish because they had ventured to another house without permission. Another man was clubbed to death because a woman had had a bad dream about him. Yet during this period of slavery, Cabeza de Vaca loosed the bonds that had held him to European ways and began to assimilate into the Indian way of life, one of the first Europeans to do so. His observations are worthy of an ethnologist. He noted that his captors slept on animal skins, that in the spring they went from the island to the mainland to pick blackberries, and that when a child died, 'the parents and the relatives and all the rest of the people weep. And the weeping lasts a whole year, that is, each day in the morning before sunrise, first the parents begin to weep, and after this the whole community weeps'.

At a time when half of this community had died of Spanish disease, there must have been wholesale mourning going on. Cabeza de Vaca also noticed how ineffective the Indian doctors were—their main cure consisted of placing hot stones on the abdomens of those who were ill and then blowing on the sick person to 'expel the disease from him'. Cabeza de Vaca and the others derided this approach, but then the Indians took their food away until the Spanish agreed to try to become healers. And of all the Spanish, it seems that Cabeza de Vaca was the most successful. His practice was to whisper prayers, make the sign of the cross and blow gently on the patient's forehead and about his body.

Apparently, this worked, or worked enough for the Indians to keep Cabeza de Vaca alive, despite the fact that he himself suffered from a severe illness and nearly died. For the next year, he was taken back and forth from the island to the mainland with the nomadic Indians. Much to his chagrin, those Spanish remaining in the group led by Dorantes and Castillo had been allowed to leave their captors and travel west along the coast, while Cabeza de Vaca and one other Spaniard, Lope de Oviedo, remained enslaved. Finally, Cabeza de Vaca escaped and made his way 'to those who live in the forests on the mainland', a tribe called the Charrucos, whom he had met while wandering with his Indian captors. He began working among them as an itinerant trader, which made him a valuable person, although also one whose life was precarious because the various Indian tribes he travelled among were almost always at war with each other.

Yet here, too, he learned a great deal about Indian cultures. Travelling for about 150 kilometres (95 miles) up the coast, he carried the items that the Indians valued—red ochre paint, the hearts of animals, seashells, pearls, flints, glue and hard cane for making arrows. For the next two years, he plied his trade, happy because 'practising it, I had the freedom to go wherever I wanted'. In fact, the only reason he did not start off for Mexico was that Oviedo remained behind on Malhado and would not leave. But finally, in the spring of 1533, Oviedo agreed to go with him.

'Three Men Like Us'

Travelling along the Gulf coast, Cabeza de Vaca and Lope de Oviedo encountered an Indian tribe who told them, much to their astonishment, that 'three men like us' were alive farther up the coast, near the lower part of what is now the state of Texas' Guadalupe River. However, the Indians who told them this also taunted the Spanish, pointing arrows at them and telling them that other white men had also been alive but had been killed merely on a whim of their captors.

This information was so frightening to Oviedo that he insisted on returning to Malhado with some Indian women he met, and thus he vanishes from history. But Cabeza de Vaca continued onward and, much to his surprise and joy, met up with Alonso del Castillo and Andrés Dorantes, along with Dorantes' North African slave, Estabancio. These men were slaves of two different Indian tribes who had gathered on the banks of the Guadalupe to pick the wild pecans that grew in great abundance.

These Spaniards were amazed to see Cabeza de Vaca alive and agreed that they would find a way to escape together. In the meantime, Cabeza de Vaca was given as a slave to the Mariames Indians, who owned Dorantes; the other two men were owned by a neighbouring tribe called the Yguazes.

Children of the Sun

The Indians with whom the Spaniards lived moved nomadically from the pecan harvests along the Guadalupe about 150 kilometres (95 miles) south to the Nueces River, where they feasted on prickly pears. The Spanish secretly agreed that at the next prickly pear festival they would escape, join up and make their way to New Spain. Cabeza de Vaca anxiously awaited this moment, but also captured mental snapshots of life in the American southwest as it had been going on for hundreds of years—the hunts where Indian men, beating wooden clappers, drove deer into the water, the vast herds of bison (Cabeza de Vaca and his friends were the first Europeans to see them), and the drunken feasts of the Mariames, who loved to dance and also to tell tall tales.

After six months, the Spaniards arrived in the land of the prickly pears, but they were unable to effect their escape because the tribes they belonged to got into a dispute and went off in different directions. Much to his horror, Cabeza de Vaca now had to wait another six months. Dorantes was now with another tribe and Cabeza de Vaca was alone. 'During this time I endured a very bad life', he wrote in his *Relación*, 'as much because of my great hunger as because of the bad treatment I received from the Indians, which was such that I had to flee three times'.

Finally, in the autumn of 1531, the Spanish reunited again, and this time they made good their escape. They found another, less hostile, tribe and were allowed to live among them as free men that winter before they headed off in the general direction of what they thought was New Spain. Gradually, the Spanish began to work as healers again, Cabeza de Vaca prominent among them. It is difficult to know why they had the success that they did—perhaps there were Indians afflicted with psychosomatic diseases, or perhaps they were suggestible to placebo, or maybe Cabeza de Vaca had some real cures up his sleeve.

Whatever happened, the men began to gain a following of Indians, who called the Spanish 'children of the sun'. Cabeza de Vaca writes: 'Among all these people it was taken for certain that we came from the sky, because all the things that they do not have or do not know the origin of, they say come from the sky'.

The Indians would creep into the Spanish campsites at dawn, with their fingers pointing to the sky. Then they rubbed their hands, with some astonishment, over the bodies of the Spanish, before bringing their sick to be cured. Gradually, the Spanish developed a method, almost as if they were doctors in a modern medical practice together. Estabancio acted as the receptionist/nurse, screening patients and finding out what ailed them. Dorantes, Castillo and Cabeza de Vaca held themselves deliberately aloof, so as to increase their mystique, before seeing their patients. They generally cured their patients by making the sign of the cross or praying over them, but also by blowing on them. Once Cabeza de Vaca even successfully performed surgery, using a knife to remove an arrowhead from a man's chest. The healers took their payment in food and also, probably, women, although in a manuscript subject to censorship by the Inquisition, Cabeza de Vaca does not explicitly state this.

Thus the healers trekked from Indian group to Indian group as they made their way in a southwesterly direction, across the Rio Grande and into northern Mexico. They began to meet trading caravans, large groups of a hundred or so Indians carrying copper and woollen goods. Everywhere the Europeans went, they were followed by a permanent band of men and women, who acted as their disciples. The Spanish started down the Mexican peninsula on the Gulf side but were dissuaded by the Indians who followed them, because they said that 'bad Indians' lived there. So, instead, Cabeza de Vaca and his men followed a meandering semicircle through northern Mexico before heading south again, on the Pacific side of New Spain.

Then, one day, Cabeza de Vaca saw an Indian wearing an amulet that was made from the belt buckle of a sword scabbard. Through the buckle was a horseshoe nail. It was the first sign of anything Spanish he had seen in eight years.

'American by Experience'

One day in the spring of 1536, in what is now the northern Mexican state of Sonora, a group of Spanish slavers rode out to capture Indians—an easy task, for the natives could never outrun their horses. These slavers saw a band of about a dozen Indians moving across the plain and raced toward them, expecting them to flee. But these Indians were different. Instead of running, they turned toward the Spanish and approached them. One of the Indians, a short, dark man with hair down to his waist and a beard that hung almost to his belt, shocked the slavers by greeting them in perfect

Spanish. The men 'remained looking at me for a long time', Cabeza de Vaca later wrote, 'so astonished that they neither talked to me nor managed to ask me anything'.

Cabeza de Vaca was finally able to explain who he and his companions were, and shocked the slavers even more by refusing to allow them to take the Indians as prisoners. This infuriated the Spanish, who through an interpreter told the Indians that Cabeza de Vaca and his fellows were Christians like themselves—implying, ironically enough, that they were just as cruel and rapacious. But the Indians did not believe this—a great testament to Cabeza de Vaca and his friends, who were probably the only Europeans on the North American continent who did not try to convert the Indians.

When Cabeza de Vaca left his little band behind, they were weeping. He and his companions entered Mexico City on 23 July 1536, to a heroes' welcome. About a year later, Cabeza de Vaca arrived home, where he immediately beseeched King Charles to give him a patent to explore the lands he had just wandered through. But despite the fact that Cabeza de Vaca seems to have hinted that there was treasure to be found in *La Florida*—he may have done this to make himself more valuable—Charles had already decided to grant the patent to Hernando de Soto. Finally, in 1540, he made Cabeza de Vaca governor of the area of the Rio de Plata in South America, but there, because he refused to allow the Indians to be enslaved and because he was increasingly difficult to get along with, he alienated his men and was shipped back to Spain on corruption charges, which were almost certainly trumped up.

Cabeza de Vaca spent much of the rest of his life disentangling himself from this mess and restoring his reputation, which he was finally able to do. He died in 1559, having penned his *Relación*, in which he no longer pretended that there was treasure to be found in the lands he had wandered through. Instead, he simply told his tale as he knew it, one of the most amazing first encounter stories in North American history. Cabeza de Vaca and his comrades were, as Andres Resendez writes, forced to 'find a middle ground' each time they came upon a new native group. They could not rely on force of arms. They were, as Resendez also writes, 'European and African by birth, but becoming American by experience'.

CHAPTER FIVE

Traversing the Amazon
Francisco de Orellana and the
unexpected river

One of the greatest journeys of exploration the world has ever known was undertaken unintentionally by desperate men. The ragged band of conquistadors led by Francisco de Orellana was in search of food and safe harbour when they inadvertently entered the fast-flowing stream of the Amazon River. Some 6000 kilometres (3700 miles) later, their rough-hewn boats wallowed in the swells of the Atlantic Ocean. They had been chased by savage Indians, attacked (or so they claimed) by women warriors, and seen all manner of strange and exotic flora and fauna. But the river itself may have been the most extraordinary sight of all—flowing swiftly along, sometimes so wide its banks could be barely discerned, often so deep that no bottom could be sounded.

When Orellana finally returned to Spain with word of his wondrous voyage he expected to be backed for a second expedition to exploit this mighty waterway, the longest in the world. Instead, he was called a traitor in certain circles and shunned by the Spanish court. When at last he was given permission to return to Brazil, it was with the most parsimonious of royal support. The result would be the tragedy he had avoided on his first trip—as the Amazon historian Anthony Smith would later write: '[The expedition] started disastrously and ended that way'.

But that was in the future. In August 1542, when Francisco de Orellana smelled the ocean breeze and felt the fresh salty splatter of the waves against his body, he knew that he had undertaken a journey no European ever had.

El Dorado

Not a great deal is known about the early life of Francisco de Orellana, but initially he followed a pattern similar to that of Cortés, Pizarro and other conquistadors. He was born in 1511 in Extremadura, that breeding ground of hard-fisted, gimlet-eyed Spanish fighters, and probably arrived in the New

World in 1527, when he was sixteen. It appears that Orellana was a relative of the Pizarro brothers, probably a second cousin, and so when he crossed the ocean he ended up joining Francisco Pizarro in Panama, and he was with Pizarro when he journeyed to Peru and engaged in his epic conquest of the Inca there. In fact, Orellana distinguished himself, fighting bravely in battles at Lima, Trujillo and Cuzco and losing an eye to a stone hurled by an Inca slinger.

He fought so well that, in 1538, six years after the death of Atahualpa, he was ordered by Francisco Pizarro to pacify the province of La Culata. Orellana made quick work of the Inca rebels there and even founded the city of Santiago de Guayaquil (modern Guayaquil, Ecuador). In 1539, Pizarro appointed him captain-general and lieutenant-governor of that city, as well as of another nearby town. Orellana was now all of twenty-eight years old and had done quite well for himself. He was far too young to retire—not something most conquistadors took easily to, in any event—and began searching around for new adventures. One presented itself when Gonzalo Pizarro, youngest of the Pizarro brothers and governor of several provinces, including La

Culata, decided to mount an expedition in search of a king named El Dorado. El Dorado was supposedly a chief of a certain tribe of Indians to the east of Peru; each year, he covered himself in gold dust and then dove into a crystal-clear mountain lake. After centuries of such a ritual, the lake was now filled with molten gold.

Far-fetched? Certainly, to our ears. But Pizarro and Orellana and the other conquistadors lived in a world where, in the previous twenty years, two fabulously wealthy and almost otherworldly civilisations, those of the Mexica and the Inca, had been discovered. Who would have thought the likes of Montezuma and Atahualpa existed? So why not a lake of gold? Governor Francisco Pizarro gave his permission for such an expedition—at the very least, it would rid him of bored and restless conquistadors who stirred up no end of trouble while idle—and Francisco de Orellana had himself invited along.

'The Limits of the Ancient Empire'

Gonzalo Pizarro set off from the high northern Inca city of Quito late in February 1541, in the company of 250 Spaniards and four thousand Inca captives—

these latter had been kept in shackles right up until the day of the march. Accompanying the human beings were two thousand pigs (for eating) and two thousand dogs (for hunting Indians), as well as horses and llamas. All told, it was quite a procession that travelled east into unknown territory in search of the lake of gold. But Gonzalo Pizarro was hedging his bets. It was not only gold he was after, but *la canela*—cinnamon. He claimed that he had been told 'by very prominent and aged chiefs' of the existence of vast forests of cinnamon trees, an extremely valuable spice back home in Spain. And so Gonzalo wrote to the King of Spain just before setting off: 'I [have] been made to believe that from these provinces [will] be obtained great treasures whereby your Majesty would be served ...'

Francisco de Orellana wanted to obtain these great treasures as well, but he did not leave Quito with Gonzalo. He had been late raising his group of conquistadors (Francisco Pizarro's permission did not mean he provided funding—Orellana had to pay for his own soldiers). When he finally arrived in Quito from Guayaquil with a much smaller group (only twenty-five soldiers and a few Indians), the citizens of that city warned him not to follow Gonzalo—they could smell disaster. They warned him that he was heading 'to the limits of the Ancient Empire of the Incas', where there were many warlike Indians of whom even the mighty Inca had been wary.

But Orellana, true *hidalgo* that he was, ignored them and marched east with his small group of men. They followed the massive trail left behind by Gonzalo and his men. A blind man could not have missed it—the countryside was littered with dead Inca and animals and scattered equipment, and there was not an iota of food to be had. In fact, Gonzalo had made an epic march. Heading into the western foothills of the Andes, he and his party experienced a tremendous earthquake, followed by torrential rains, thunder and lightning. After that they made a dangerous crossing of this rugged mountain chain, at heights up to 3000 metres (10,000 feet). It was here that many of the Inca captives began to die off, of exposure and malnutrition. Gonzalo finally came down into the dense jungles on the eastern slopes of the mountains and began wandering, seeking El Dorado and *la canela*. The latter he actually found, but the trees were of such poor quality that he gave up the search for cinnamon and began torturing local Indian chiefs—tearing them apart with dogs was a favoured tactic—attempting to get them to reveal the location of El Dorado.

It was at this point that Francisco de Orellana caught up with him. It had been a rough journey for him and his men, for not only was there no food along Gonzalo's path, but he had thoroughly alienated the local Indians with his rough treatment and these had taken out their frustrations on Orellana's smaller and more vulnerable group with numerous ambushes. When he finally staggered into Gonzalo's camp, he had left 'only a sword and a shield, and his companions likewise'.

But Gonzalo was quite happy to see him. He embraced him and made him his lieutenant-general, second-in-command of the expedition.

River Crossroads

The conquistadors were now in a country of deep jungle. The Andes rising behind them caught and pushed back all the moisture in the air, so that it rained continually as the Spanish drove deeper into the forest—their clothes simply rotted off their backs. They were horrified by the huge snakes that slithered through the forest and were plagued by unrelenting heat and disease-carrying mosquitoes. Here the Inca began to die off in earnest, of various tropical diseases as well as overwork. The conquistadors captured whatever Indians they could find and forced them to act as guides, but these Indians often led the expedition astray or escaped, leaving it lost. The pigs having now all died, the Spanish were reduced to eating herbs, roots and wild fruits as they cut their way through deep vegetation, following the banks of a fast-flowing river that finally led into the Napo River, a tributary—although the Spanish did not know this—of the mighty Amazon.

Eyes watched the Spanish from the forest as they stumbled along, but these watching natives disappeared when the Spanish attempted to capture them. Those Indians unlucky enough to be caught had by now learned how savage these bearded invaders were and so repeated the same mantra—pointing down the Napo, they claimed that this mysterious golden king lived in *that* direction (anywhere but here). But at this point the Spanish, reduced to eating lizards and now dying off themselves, simply wanted to find food.

Seeing Indians in their fleet canoes and realising that the rivers they increasingly encountered were the highways through this wilderness, the Spanish stopped and built a rough boat, which they called a brigantine. They put those who were the weakest aboard the ship, which was paddled down the Napo while the stronger conquistadors pushed their way through the jungles on the banks.

Soon even this halting progress became impossible. With more and more of the men sickening, Gonzalo Pizarro halted the party and held a conference on the banks of the Napo. They had heard of a great river and a wealthy country about ten days' journey away, but such were the dire straits of the expedition that Pizarro was certain that most of the men would not be able to make it that far. By now it was not gold that Pizarro was after, simply food and shelter. Francisco de Orellana then suggested a solution—that he take a group of men down the river in the brigantine, find this wealthy land and bring back supplies to the rest of them. Pizarro thought long and hard about this, and decided to acquiesce. On 26 December 1541, Orellana left the camp with fifty-nine men and the brigantine. Pizarro and 140 men stayed behind.

The Village of Plenty

Orellana and his small party paddled for nine days—a distance of perhaps 1000 kilometres (620 miles)—with the swift currents becoming swifter, moving them farther and farther away from Pizarro and the stranded expedition. At one point, an underwater log stove in the bottom of the boat, but they repaired it and continued, desperate to find food, eating forest roots and gnawing on pieces of leather. In early January they heard, in the distance, the unnerving sound of heavy, incessant drumming. At first they thought that this was an auditory hallucination brought on by the delirium caused by their fevers, but as the river carried them along, they realised it was real. Orellana insisted that they put on armour and man a watch as the river coursed through unrelenting jungle. The drumming grew louder and then they rounded a bend and came upon four canoes full of Indians, who turned and paddled away as fast as they could. Orellana and his men gave chase.

In a short while they came upon a village, which was deserted but did contain food. The men set about eating 'with so much eagerness that they thought they would never satisfy themselves'. Even so, they were wary, 'their shields on their shoulders and their swords under their arms'. Finally, the Indians, who had been watching from the jungle, returned, and here we can see the difference between the command styles of Francisco de Orellana and Gonzalo Pizarro. Instead of immediately attacking the natives, Orellana, who had troubled to learn some of the local languages, gave them gifts and asked politely for more food in return, which the Indians brought. The next day, Orellana addressed a gathering of the Indian chiefs and claimed the land for the King of Spain. No one knows how much of this the Indians understood, but they did understand that this Spaniard was not attempting to have semi-feral dogs chew them to death, and so they responded with hospitality for the bearded strangers.

Having rested for a while, Orellana and his men were faced with what was literally a life or death choice: to return to Gonzalo Pizarro and the rest of the expedition, or to push on to the huge river that the Indians assured them lay ahead.

Controversy

The dilemma was clear to everyone in the party. They had promised to return with food and supplies for their suffering comrades back upriver, but they had barely survived themselves—had paddled for days through a 'foodless country' until they came to the sound of drums and the village of plenty. To paddle back upstream through this same country would take them twice as long, since they would be moving against the swift current. They would certainly run out of any supplies they had with them, more of them would die—seven of Orellana's men had already perished on their journey downstream—and they would arrive unable to help Pizarro's men, who, no doubt, were already dying off.

The only sensible decision to make, if they wanted to survive, was to move on. Yet this was a powerful and emotional step to take, because they knew (or assumed) that they would be leaving their friends and comrades to die back there in the endless rain and pestilential jungle. Orellana, although he was pragmatic enough to realise that they needed to move on, offered to take his men back to Pizarro, but this was probably merely so that he could later say that he had offered to return. The men in any event refused. Among them was a Dominican priest, Friar Gaspar de Carvajal, who was keeping the main record of the expedition. He wrote that the men 'swore by the sign of the Cross and the four sacred Gospels' that they wanted Orellana to lead them onward. And so Orellana acquiesced.

However, Gonzalo Pizarro would not see things in quite the same light and did his best to brand Orellana a traitor for not coming back, claiming that he displayed 'the greatest cruelty that ever faithless men have shown'. This was a smear job that has lasted for hundreds of years. Ultimately, while it is only natural that Pizarro would feel Orellana's failure to return as a betrayal, moving ahead was the only responsible decision that Orellana could make, given the circumstances.

'To Guide Us to the Sea'

Once the decision had been made, Orellana turned to practical matters. He was certain the mighty river just ahead would take them out into the Atlantic Ocean on the east coast of Brazil—in fact, he assumed it would be but a short distance before they encountered ocean waves. But the boat they were currently using would simply fall apart in the rough Atlantic swells, 'if God saw fit to guide us to the sea', as Carvajal wrote. Therefore, Orellana told the men they needed to build a bigger and better boat. This seemed a nearly impossible task, in the middle of the wilderness, for men who were not shipbuilders but, as Carvajal wrote, two men approached Orellana and said they could build a blacksmith's forge to make nails from odd bits of metal and old horseshoes. Another journal-keeper, the conquistador Antonio de Herrera, wrote that 'timber for the ship was cut and prepared with great labour, which the men endured with much willingness, and in thirty-five days she was launched, caulked with cotton, and the seams filled with pitch which was given to them by the Indians'.

On 4 April, Orellana and his men set off down the Napo. For a month, they passed through seemingly uninhabited wilderness, with the jungle coming right down to the banks. Then the river grew wider and so fast moving that they were unable to fish as they coursed along. Without realising it, they had entered the Amazon—the longest river in the world (although disputed recent measurements have the Nile beating it by a nose)—which contains one-fifth of the world's fresh water supply and runs 6000 kilometres (4000 miles) to the Atlantic Ocean. The river is so wide it is often called the

'River Sea' and contains islands the size of small countries. The first European to see the Amazon was the Spanish explorer Vicente Pinzón, who sailed into its mouth in 1500—the Amazon's estuary is some 400 kilometres (250 miles) wide—but no white person had ever traversed its entire length.

Orellana and the expedition were a fascinating sight to the Indians of the Amazon basin. Not only did the men fill the larger and newer ship they had built, but they also brought along the older one, as well as numerous dugout canoes they had stolen or traded for with the locals they encountered. In May, they were told by Indians they met that they were approaching the territory of a powerful chief named Machiparo, who held sway over some fifty thousand people. They proceeded cautiously and one morning, according to Carvajal, saw in the distance villages 'gleaming white' in the sun. All at once, the river was filled:

… with a great many canoes, all equipped for fighting [and] gaily-coloured. [The warriors in them] carried shields which are made of the shell-like skins of lizards and the hides of manatees and tapirs, as tall as a man, for they cover them entirely. They were coming

on with a great yell, playing on many drums and
wooden trumpets, threatening us as if they were going
to devour us.

Orellana knew that the time for combat was at hand. He ordered the two brigantines to be lashed together and told everyone onboard both boats to make ready with their crossbows and harquebuses. Then the men watched in grim silence as the canoes of the Indians dashed toward them, coming on 'in such an orderly fashion and with so much arrogance that it seemed as if they already had us in their hands'. When the lead canoes got close enough, Orellana gave the order to fire but, unfortunately, the gunpowder was wet and would not ignite. The battle was left to the crossbowmen, who shot their iron bolts into the enemy, knocking Indians into the water and causing the canoes to retreat momentarily. But soon they came on again, full of screaming warriors.

Running for Their Lives
Thus began an epic chase down the fast waters of the Amazon, with the Spanish fighting off wave after wave of canoes full of Indians, who appeared

to want to board the brigantines. After some time of this, Orellana decided that he needed to land at a village, both to get supplies and to create defensive positions to fight off the harrying Indians. It was a bold decision, for after they beached the boats the party was besieged both from land and sea. It is a sign of how hungry the Spanish were that even as they were fighting they were amassing the considerable foodstuffs of one of Machiparo's villages—turtles (kept by the tribes in pens), meat, fish and biscuits made of cornmeal. Yet the fighting on land was so fierce that eighteen of the Spanish were wounded. Deciding to retreat back to the boats, Orellana carried the wounded wrapped up in blankets, so that they looked like sacks of looted corn and the enemy would not know they had hurt them.

Back on the river, the expedition headed downstream, but their relief at escape was to be short-lived. Each time they passed a village, the men would leap into their canoes and come out to fight the Spanish with arrows and blowpipes, before falling behind, and then another village would send its own canoes out. The Spanish fought contin-uously until they were 'thoroughly exhausted' and

Orellana felt compelled to put in to shore again, this time on an uninhabited island, in order to feed and rest his soldiers. But no sooner did they light their cooking fires than the Indians were attacking again, and after several skirmishes Orellana ordered the boats back in the water and the chases began all over again. Carvajal noticed that shamans had begun to appear among the Indians, 'There went about among these men and the war canoes four or five sorcerers, all daubed with whitewash and with their mouths full of ashes, which they blew into the air … as a form of enchantment'.

The enchantment, whatever it was, nearly worked. With Indian canoes chasing them, they entered a narrow part of the river that was overlooked by high banks. Indians lined both sides of it, while the canoes closed in behind the Spanish. It was obviously going to be a tough spot to escape from, but then the expedition had a bit of luck. On shore, waving his arms and yelling, was a man who was the obvious leader of this tribe. Finding his powder at last dry, one Spanish harquebusier took careful aim, fired, and hit the man right in the chest. His warriors were so astonished at the blast and the death of their chief that they were distracted and the Spanish escaped. Finally, after two more days and nights of running fights, they found themselves free of their tormentors.

But only momentarily.

'In a Country so Well-peopled'

Riding down the Amazon was turning out to be akin to running a gauntlet. The area was much more heavily populated than they would have imagined—according to Carvajal, in some sections there was barely a crossbow shot's distance between villages. (Scientists for centuries have disputed Carvajal's description, thinking that the soil of the Amazon basin, beneath its triple-canopied jungle, is simply too poor, too deprived of nutrients and sunlight, to support such large populations. But recent studies have shown that Carvajal was probably accurate in his depiction—human beings once inhabited the Amazon jungle, especially along the rivers, in much larger numbers than they do now.)

As soon as the Spanish left the country of Machiparo they came into the land of another great chief, Omagua. At the first village they came to the warriors were lined up, ready to get into their canoes and attack, but finally Orellana had had enough. In true conquistador fashion, he decided to launch a pre-emptive strike. Landing at the village, his men charged into the Indians, slaughtering them ruthlessly and driving them away from their homes. The village was fortified with a palisade and the Spanish made good use of this to drive off attackers while they rested and ate.

It was now, according to Carvajal's diary, 16 May 1542 and the men had come, they estimated, 340 leagues (about 2000 kilometres or 1200 miles). Getting into their boats again, they wearily moved onward. The river became wider and wider and the Spanish sailed as far into midstream as possible, to avoid surprise attacks. In early June they came upon the River Negro, whose dark waters formed a visible black slash into the Amazon that could be seen for kilometres. They began to notice that they were in a more civilised countryside. Some of the villages contained 'villas' with fine plates, bowls, goblets and candelabra made of glass and a kind of porcelain. There was also a fair amount of gold and silver. From these villages ran what Carvajal called 'many roads [and] fine highways to the inland country'. Orellana ventured down one of these roads, which after a short while became 'more like a royal highway [in Spain]'. (Once again, these depictions were, until only recently, thought to be fanciful, but there is increasing evidence of sophisticated Amazonian civilisations about which we know next to nothing.)

Interestingly enough, seeing this broad highway caused the intrepid conquistador to return quickly to the boats, thinking it not 'prudent' to advance any farther. Had Orellana been stronger and had his men been in better shape, such a highway might have meant the road to a city of gold, as it had with the Inca and Mexica. But Orellana now was after not shining spires but, as Carvajal put it, 'discovery' of a different type—meaning rescue and safety. The Spanish now never spent the night ashore. 'In a country so well-peopled,' wrote Carvajal, 'it was not advisable to remain on shore during the night'.

'The Excellent Land of the Amazons'

Not long after they passed the River Negro, the conquistadors had the encounter that would make their trip notorious in history and give the great river they travelled its name. One morning, they landed at one village where the Indians did not try to attack them. These people told them that they were forced to pay tribute in parrot feathers to a tribe of fierce women who ruled the area. Can this have been true? It is hard to say. One wonders, really, how much of the language the Spanish understood and also whether or not it was possible that the Indians were kidding them, having perhaps heard that the Spanish, while fierce themselves, were credulous—innocents, as far as the seasoned Amazonian Indians were concerned. But as they journeyed farther downstream, the Spanish heard more and more tales of ferocious warrior women. Without yet encountering them, they began to refer to them as Amazons, after the fighting women of Greek myth who lived in what is now the Ukraine.

While no Amazons appeared as yet, the Spanish began to travel through an area terrifying in appearance. As they sped past on the current they saw, in one village, seven gibbets on which, according to Carvajal, were nailed 'many dead men's heads'. Another village appeared to be deserted, but when the Spanish approached it, five thousand warriors leaped from hiding—an obvious trap. At one point they captured an 'Indian girl of much intelligence', who told them that 'Christians like ourselves' were held captive in the interior.

Carvajal speculated that these were the survivors of a shipwreck, but the party did not feel able to rescue them and they pressed forward. (No proof of Christians living in the Amazon at that time has ever been found.)

Now at last, says Carvajal, 'we came suddenly upon the excellent land and dominion of the Amazons'. Being forced to put into a village for food, Orellana attempted to trade with the Indians, but they mocked him and told the Spanish they were to be captured and taken to the Amazons. A fierce fight broke out and the Spanish were barely holding their own when suddenly about a dozen women fighters appeared, fighting 'so courageously that the Indians did not dare to turn their backs; anyone who did turn their back [the Amazons] killed with clubs right there before us'.

These fierce women, Carvajal wrote, 'are very white and tall, and have their hair very long, and braided and wound about their head, and they are very robust, and go about naked, with just their privy parts covered, doing as much fighting as ten Indian men'. They wielded powerful bows. In fact, the women shot so many arrows into the brigantines that they looked 'like porcupines'. Fortunately, says

Carvajal, 'the Lord was pleased to give strength to our companions, who killed seven or eight' of the women, and the Spanish escaped.

This was their last encounter with the Amazons (although Carvajal would describe in great detail the customs of these women) but, in a sense, they would steal the thunder of Orellana's great journey. Although his men had begun to call the great river Orellana's River—and, in fact, it appears this way on European maps for some years after—it soon became commonly known as the Amazon.

'So Great Was the Joy We Felt'

The expedition passed out of the land of the Amazons, but continued to have to fight its way down the river. In one of many skirmishes, an arrow pierced the eye of Gaspar de Carvajal and 'went through to the other side', as he wrote. 'I have lost the eye and [even now] I am not without suffering … although Our Lord, without my deserving it, has been kind enough to grant me life so that I may mend my ways and serve him better.'

Despite this grievous injury, Carvajal 'rejoiced not a little' with the rest of the men when they suddenly felt the pulling of the tide, meaning that they were nearing the sea. On most rivers the tides do not extend far inland but, of course, the Amazon was different—they were still fairly far upstream when they felt this pull. Nonetheless, the expedition stopped to make the vessels as fit as possible for the ocean voyage they were facing, and then continued on for days. Finally, on 7 August 1542—St Louis' Day—'we passed out of the mouth of the river', as Carvajal put it, and into the ocean. They had been nine months on the Amazon. Amazingly, only three of Orellana's men had been killed. Both brigantines then set sail north, up the coast of Brazil. Despite being separated for nine days, they reunited in Trinidad, safe at last. 'So great was the joy we felt', wrote Carvajal, 'that I shall not be able to express it'.

Leaving his men behind, Francisco de Orellana caught a ship to take him back across the Atlantic and made his report to King Charles of Spain, hoping to get royal backing for a return trip to really explore the Amazon interior. But back in Quito, Gonzalo Pizarro—having survived an arduous trip of his own—was writing a letter accusing Orellana of high treason. There were many who felt Orellana had betrayed Pizarro by leaving him there to die, while others believed he took the only course of action open to him. The result was that Charles did sponsor Orellana for another expedition to Brazil, but in half-hearted fashion. His ships were poor, his sailors lacked experience, and his supplies were deficient. By the time he arrived at the mouth of the Amazon around Christmas 1545, he had lost some ninety sailors to sickness.

Even so, Orellana headed upriver for 100 leagues. Now the scenario repeated itself: his men began to starve and die—fifty-seven more died during his three months' sailing up the great river—and Orellana went off with a small party to find food for them. There ensued months of grievous wanderings as the party was whittled down by disease, starvation and hostile Indians. A few men managed to patch together boats and sail them back to Trinidad, much as Orellana had three years earlier. Francisco de Orellana was not with them, however. He had died of disease deep in the jungle, having succumbed, finally, to the irresistible but deadly pull of the Amazon.

CHAPTER SIX

Savage Meetings in an Unforgiving Wilderness
Henry Hudson and the search for the northern passage

On a frigid June day in 1611, in a salty bay still filled with ice and surrounded by frozen wilderness, one of the great explorers of the Age of Exploration was forcibly placed in a small boat, along with his son and seven other sickly men. They were given a little powder and shot, and some rope, and a small amount of food, and then the line tying them to the larger ship they had come from—the *Discovery*—was severed.

The explorer's name was Henry Hudson and he had just been abandoned by his mutinous crew. This was not like being cut loose in the balmy seas of the South Pacific. He was in the large saltwater gulf that Hudson had thought would carry him to the Northwest Passage he sought and that would soon be named after him: Hudson Bay. But there was nowhere for his small boat to go and little sustenance, and he and his young son and the other men aboard would surely die of hunger or exposure, which was, in fact, the intention of the mutineers. Aboard the *Discovery*, they quickly set sail and fled, one later wrote, 'as if from an enemy'. Hudson set his small boat's sail and chased them for a time, but the larger vessel quickly outdistanced him and the last the mutineers—or anyone—saw of Henry Hudson was his bearded, impassive figure staring after them with gaunt eyes as his little ship fell farther and farther behind.

Northeast Passage

Henry Hudson springs full-blown into history in 1607 and then disappears (literally) four years later, having made four exploration voyages that opened up the river, strait and bay named after him. We know almost nothing about his life before this. He was born in London in about 1570 and probably began going to sea relatively young, as a cabin boy, and then worked his way up to master. Along the way he married a woman named Katherine—we do not have her maiden name—who bore him three sons: Richard, John and Oliver. Hudson became sought after as a captain and navigator; it was probably the latter skill, in particular, that attracted the attention of the English Muscovy Company. In the early seventeenth century, the big merchant companies, particularly the Dutch and English ones, sought a northern passage to Asia that would preclude their vessels having to sail southern waters, either through the Strait of Magellan or around the Cape of Good Hope. This was partly because of the distances involved and partly because they wanted to avoid the hostile and proprietary navies of Spain and Portugal, which patrolled the New World and the routes to the Spice Islands.

The English Muscovy Company, more colloquially known as the Russia Company, traded with Russia and so sought a Northeast Passage that would lead to Russia's northern ports and also down the Pacific Ocean to China. They signed up Henry Hudson to make the search for such a passage, giving him a small crew and a vessel, the *Hopewell*, and sending him off in May 1607. Hudson subscribed to the theory that the three months of constant summer daylight around the northern waters of Russia would melt the ice and allow a free water passage, but he was sorely mistaken. On this first voyage he sailed north between Greenland and Spitzbergen and actually came within ten degrees of the North Pole—closer than anyone had ever been—before turning east, but massive pack ice forced him back.

It was a valiant effort and the Russia Company signed him up again to repeat the voyage in 1609, but this time he got little farther. He was, in fact, attempting the impossible—there exists a Northeast Passage, but for ships of Hudson's day it would not have been navigable. Still, he persisted in trying to convince the Russia Company to hire him again for yet a third voyage. When they declined, he offered his services to the Vereenigde Oostindische Compagnie (VOC), the Dutch East India Company.

The Half Moon

After some trepidation—Hudson's star had been tarnished by his failed two previous voyages—the VOC hired Hudson to make another attempt to press through to the Northeast Passage. However, he had apparently told the officers of the VOC that it was his real belief that a way through to Asia was to be found in the northwest, across North America. He based this in good part on letters from his friend John Smith, the English explorer who had helped settle Virginia Colony, who told him that he thought there existed, somewhere north of Virginia, a strait that led to Asia.

The VOC officials refused to allow Hudson to explore west and he agreed to this proscription, but one wonders if it was in the back of his mind when he set sail from Amsterdam on his third voyage, on 6 May 1609. He was aboard a tiny vessel— described in his VOC contract as a 'yacht'—called the *Half Moon* and had with him a crew of eighteen, including, significantly, a fifty-year-old mariner from London whose name was Robert Juet. Juet, a surly malcontent, was to figure prominently in Hudson's life and in history, too, for Hudson's log of his famous third voyage has mainly disappeared and it is only Juet's accounts that we have.

From Amsterdam, the *Half Moon* sailed up the west coast of Norway, rounded what is called the North Cape, and then headed east into the Barents Sea. Hudson soon found himself at Novaya Zemlya, an island group that juts out from the northern coast of Russia into the Arctic Ocean. In these treacherous seas he faced pack ice, violent winds, blinding snow and frigid temperatures, something the Dutch among his mixed English–Dutch crew were unfamiliar with, having spent most of their sailing time in the sunnier climes of the Dutch East Indies. Still Hudson persisted until, in mid-May, he realised he had a mutiny on his hands. His men refused to sail the ship a league farther and demanded that he turn around. Normally speaking, no self-respecting ship's master would give in to such demands—on the high seas, a ship's captain was a godlike figure in his own vessel—but it appears Hudson was prepared for the mutiny, and may even have welcomed it.

According to an account Hudson gave to Emanuel von Meteren, the Dutch lawyer who had helped connect Hudson with the VOC, Hudson brought out nautical charts to show to his mutinous crew that they should go to the American coast, 'to the latitude of about 40 degrees'. It was there, Hudson said, that 'his friend Captain Smith … informed him that there was a sea leading into the western ocean to the north of the southern English colony [Virginia]'.

This was met with general agreement and Hudson turned his ship around and headed back west through the Barents Sea. He was breaking his instructions from the VOC not to explore for a Northwest Passage, which is presumably why he did not bring the *Half Moon* to Amsterdam for refitting but instead chose to sail all the way to North America. Fighting off stormy seas—the ship lost its foremast and sail in one North Atlantic gale—the *Half Moon* arrived off the coast of Newfoundland on 3 July, spotting what Robert Juet called 'a great fleet of Frenchmen' fishing off the Outer Banks. They sailed past these vessels without trying to make contact and finally came within sight of the coast of Cape Sable, Nova Scotia, on 13 July.

Murderers

Mist shrouded the Nova Scotia shore as the *Half Moon* tried to beat its way closer, so Hudson had to hold off, lest he break up on the rocks that lined the coast. Finally, about ten o'clock in the morning, two canoes carrying 'six of the savages of the country', as Juet put it, paddled out and the Indians were brought on board. They claimed to be very happy to see the *Half Moon*. They had a meal with Hudson and his crew and told them that 'there were gold, silver and copper mines hard by us, and that the Frenchmen do trade with them', something Juet found easy to believe as one or two of the Indians had a smattering of that language.

After stopping in 'a very good harbour' and cutting themselves a new foremast, the *Half Moon* and its crew were on their way again. They next stopped near the mouth of the St George's River in what is now the state of Maine, and here begins the puzzling saga of Hudson and the *Half Moon* when it comes to their contact with native people. Juet writes of a fairly peaceful scene—the crew of the *Half Moon* finding fresh water, plucking thirty-one lobsters from the sea for a fine dinner and allowing the local 'country people' (that is, the Indians) on board to trade. But then he says: 'The people coming aboard showed us great friendship, but we could not trust them'.

Why? Juet goes on to write that in the morning two more boatloads of Indians came to trade, people who 'offered us no wrong, seeing as how we stood upon our guard'. These Indians had come in French-built shallops, so it is possible that Juet thought they might attack the English (although at the time there existed no official state of hostilities between France and England). Yet the Indians somehow frightened Juet and, presumably, Hudson, for on 25 July, two days after their initial landing at St George's River, Juet writes:

We manned our boat and scout [smaller boat] with 12 men and muskets and two stone pieces or murderers [a murderer being a small, short range cannon] and drove the savages from their houses and took the spoil of them as they would have done to us. Then we set sail and came down to the harbor's mouth and rode there all night.

Why attack and rob these Indians? There is no mention of an Indian assault, no mention of any Indians stealing from the *Half Moon*, no mention of any inciting incident at all. The grimly paranoid tone of Juet's notes is frightening, almost as if insanity lurks. Yet it would seem likely that Hudson countenanced such an attack. Whatever happened, compared with the far kindlier treatment the Indians were getting at exactly that moment at the hands of Samuel de Champlain, this incident certainly put the English and Dutch in a bad light.

'A Great Stream'

The *Half Moon* continued down the coast, having cautionary encounters with the local Indians. Near what is now Cape Cod, Massachusetts, 'the voices of men' were heard shouting from the shore: 'We sent our boat on shore thinking they had been some Christians left on the land, but we found them to be savages', Juet writes, apparently unable to understand why anyone who was not a 'Christian' would call out to them. When the Indians came on board the ship, they were quite friendly, pointing out a nearby river where the Europeans could fish. Juet's description of them smacks of envy: 'The people have green tobacco and pipes, the bowls of which are made of earth and pipes of red copper. The land is very sweet.'

By 17 August, the ship had sailed far enough down the coast to reach Chesapeake Bay, where Captain John Smith had helped found Jamestown in 1607. Although they were near 'the entrance to the King's River, where our Englishmen are', Juet wrote, Hudson chose not to land there, perhaps because they were sailing under a Dutch flag. After being blown as far south as Cape Hatteras, North Carolina, in a violent storm that arose, the

Half Moon began to beat its way back north again, now closer to shore, searching for the strait to the Pacific that Smith said he thought existed. Hudson reached the mouth of the Delaware River, which had not yet been explored by any European, but shoals prevented him entering the waterway and so he continued north.

On 2 September, Juet wrote in his journal:

We saw a great fire but could not see the land. From the land which we had first sight of, until we came to a great lake of water, as we could judge it to be, being drowned land which made it rise like islands.

We had a great stream out of the bay.

What Juet was describing was the very mouth of the enormous bay that is now New York Harbor. 'The great stream out of the bay' was, in fact, what would come to be called the Hudson River.

'Ever-flowing Waters'

This great bay had, in fact, been discovered over three quarters of a century before by Giovanni da Verrazano, an Italian explorer in the employ of the

French, but he had only spent a short amount of time there and soon his discovery was forgotten. Since that time, no European had visited the bay or entered the mighty river, which was called Mahicanituk by the local Lenape Indians, meaning 'ever-flowing waters'.

Even far out to sea, the current of the Hudson River was strong and Henry Hudson was hopeful that this, at last, was the broad river that would provide passage to the Pacific Ocean. The *Half Moon* sailed New York Harbor for several days, with the crew taking depth soundings and marvelling at the incredible profusion of fish—in one afternoon they caught 'ten great mullets, of a foot and a half long apiece, and a ray as great as four men could hale into the ship'. They landed in what is now the New York borough of Staten Island and were met by Indians who were, according to Juet, very polite: 'They go in deer skins loose, well dressed. They have yellow copper … they have a great store of maize or Indian wheat, whereof they make good bread. The country is full of great and tall oaks'.

Yet, once again … the note of fear, suspicion, paranoia on the part of Juet. The Indians visited the ship and all went well, but 'at night they went on land again, so we rode very quiet, but durst not trust them'. And perhaps he was right. On the morning of 6 September, Henry Hudson sent a seaman named John Colman along with four other men to explore another river that entered the ocean about 22 kilometres (14 miles) away. The men did this, finding nothing remarkable, but when they were returning that night they encountered two canoes filled with Indians, who fired arrows at them for no apparent reason. Two sailors were slightly wounded and John Colman's throat was pierced by an arrow and he died there in the boat.

As evening came on and it began to rain, the sailors escaped their assailants but in the darkness could not find the *Half Moon*, and thus were forced to spend a terrifying night rowing about the harbour, since the current was too strong for their small anchor to gain any purchase on the bottom. The next morning they returned to the *Half Moon* and related what had happened. Hudson ordered that Colman be buried and that waist-high boards be placed around the ship's gunwales to protect against attack—but, interestingly enough, allowed on board yet another group of Indians who wanted to trade.

These Indians, said Juet, 'offered no violence', but the next day two canoes approached the *Half Moon*, filled with Indian men with bows and arrows. Could these have been the Indians who attacked Colman and his men? It is hard to say. The wary Europeans only allowed several on board and then promptly kidnapped them, although one leaped overboard and swam away. Having decided that enough was enough, Hudson weighed anchor and sailed into the upper bay of New York Harbor and then into the Hudson River, anchoring for the night off a hilly, thickly wooded island the Lenapes called 'Manna-hata'.

In Search of the Passage

The next morning, the *Half Moon* travelled up the river that would one day bear Hudson's name. The Hudson River is really a huge estuary, with the water salty as far as 100 kilometres (60 miles) inland and tides extending for half its 510-kilometre (315-mile) length up into northern New York State. At first Hudson and the crew of the *Half Moon* were extremely excited. A few miles north of Manna-hata, around the area that became known as the Tappan Zee, the river widens to 5 kilometres

(3 miles) across and it must have begun to seem to Hudson—who had no idea of the 5000-kilometre (3000-mile) width of the American continent—like the broad strait that would take him to Asia.

As morose as ever, Juet reported more canoes approaching the ship: 'This morning there came ... eight and twenty canoes full of men, women, and children to betray us, but we saw their intent, and suffered none of them to come aboard'. It would have been highly unusual for Indians to put their women and children in harm's way during an assault. It is also more than possible that these Indians had traded with the French and assumed that these Europeans wanted to trade as well. But Juet darkly saw danger everywhere, despite the glory of the scene: the high cliffs, or Palisades, on the western side of the river, the brilliantly coloured autumn foliage of the forests falling away endlessly to the east. The sun remained out; the weather was warm. Much to Juet's chagrin, on the morning of 15 September, 'our two [kidnapped] savages got out of a porthole and swam away. After we were under sail they called to us in scorn'.

At around the same time, however, the river literally took a disturbing turn. The Hudson makes a sharp 'S' at the promontory where the United States Military Academy at West Point currently sits and then becomes much narrower and shallower. After this, it broadens out again, but in the next few days, as Hudson sailed on at an average of 30 kilometres (20 miles) a day, he could see that this waterway was almost certainly not a strait that was leading anywhere. The water was becoming more and more shallow and filled with silt and sandbars; it was apparent to him, with his vast experience, that he was reaching the headwaters of a river.

About 60 kilometres (40 miles) south of the present-day New York State capital city of Albany, Hudson stopped and allowed himself to have dinner with Indians who had sailed forth in their canoes—he tells the story in one of the few excerpts from his journal to survive:

I sailed to the shore in one of their canoes, with an old man, who was the chief of a tribe consisting of 40 men and 17 women … Two men were also despatched at once with bows and arrows in quest of game, who soon after brought in a pair of pigeons, which they had shot. They likewise killed a fat dog and skinned it in great haste with shells which they had got out of the water …

*The natives are very good people, for when they saw
that I would not remain with them [for the night],
they supposed that I was afraid of their bows, and
taking the arrows, they broke them in pieces and
threw them in the fire.*

Hudson's journal has a far more reasonable tone
than that of Robert Juet's, leading one to wonder
on what level Hudson was in control of the ship—
who was in charge, really, during their skirmishes
with the 'savages'?

'We Saw No People to Trouble Us'

After a few more days on the river, the *Half Moon*
arrived near the present-day city of Albany. The
river had definitely narrowed but, just to make
sure, Hudson sent five men up the river in the
ship's boat, to take soundings. The men returned
that night, 'in a shower of rain', Juet writes, to say
that the river 'was at an end for shipping to go in …
For they had gone eight or nine leagues [roughly
50 kilometres or 30 miles] and found but 7 foot
[2 metres] water and inconstant soundings'.

It was time to turn back. While the ship's boat
had been away, many Indians had visited the *Half*

Moon and, according to Juet, Hudson decided to find out 'whether they had any treachery in them. So they took them down into the cabin and gave them [so] much wine and Aqua Vitae that they were all merry'. This little trick, however, failed to bring out any grand plot on the part of the Indians—in fact, it just put them peacefully to sleep.

At midday on 23 September, Hudson headed the *Half Moon* south down the Hudson. All the way back, they were visited by Indians wanting to trade with them. These encounters occurred peacefully, until the ship had nearly reached Tappan Zee, at which point an Indian in a canoe pulled up to the *Half Moon*'s stern, climbed the rudder and through a stern porthole, and stole a pillow and two shirts that happened to belong to Juet. The ship's first mate shot and killed the man. Then Juet and other sailors got into the ship's boat and went to recover Juet's belongings from the canoe, at which point a swimming Indian put his hand on the gunwale of the boat, as if to overturn it. According to Juet, at this point 'our cook took a sword and cut off one of [the Indian's] hands and he was drowned'.

The final blaze of violence was to occur above the island of Manna-hata, site of the future city of New

York. According to Juet, 'one of the Indians who swam away from them' (that is, one of their former captives) led an attack against the *Half Moon*:

Two canoes full of men, with their bows and arrows shot at us after our stern. In recompense thereof we discharged six muskets and killed two or three of them. Then above a hundred came to a point of land to shoot at us.

There I shot a Falcon [a small cannon] and killed two of them whereupon the rest fled into the woods. Yet they manned off another canoe with nine or ten men which came to meet us. So I shot at it also a Falcon, and shot it through, and killed one of them. Then our men with their muskets killed three or four more.

So they went on their way and [after a while] we anchored in a bay clear of all danger of them on the other side of the river. We saw a very good piece of ground and hard by it there was a cliff that looked of the color of a white-green, as though it were either copper or silver mine ... It is on that side of the river that is called Manna-hata. We saw no people to trouble us.

A few days later, the *Half Moon* entered New York Harbor again, and then found itself in the Atlantic. And Juet wrote: 'By the seventh day of November, being Saturday, by the grace of God we safely arrived in the range of Dartmouth, in Devonshire'.

Fourth and Fatal Voyage

Although Hudson had begun his voyage contracted to the VOC, he ended it in England, for when he landed there, that November of 1609, the English government confiscated his ship and his papers and forbade him to leave the country. It appears that Hudson was able to send his Dutch employers a report on his activities—and quite a valuable one, too, for although he had failed to find a Northwest Passage (let alone a Northeast one, as he was charted to do) he had found fertile new land in America, all the time sailing under the flag of the Dutch. Within two years, the Dutch would have a settlement on the island of Manna-hata.

The English now regretted that they had not sent Hudson west themselves and soon set out to rectify that error. A group of private investors formed a company to finance Hudson's fourth voyage of discovery. His orders were to head for the poorly understood waterways of the Canadian Arctic, in order to discover 'if any passage might be found to the other ocean called the South Sea [the Pacific]'.

On 17 April 1610, Hudson set off in the ship *Discovery*, this time accompanied by his son John, perhaps ten years old, who was serving as ship's boy. Robert Juet was with him again, as first mate, as well as a passenger (perhaps hired by Hudson's employers, his status is not entirely clear) named Abacuk Prickett, who later published an account of the journey. Although fragments of Hudson's log for this fourth voyage do exist, it is mainly Prickett's story that historians have relied on.

Apparently, the voyage was fraught with tension from the beginning. Hudson fired one crewman before the ship had reached Gravesend—still on the Thames River, in other words—and hired another, Henry Greene, a young reprobate of 'lewd life and conversation', according to Prickett. Hudson may have seen Greene as a reclamation project. However, it is disturbing that this great explorer seems not to have been a great appraiser of human beings, for both Juet and Greene were to cause great trouble on this, Hudson's last, adventure.

The *Discovery* had barely reached Iceland when trouble began. Greene picked a fight with the ship's surgeon and, instead of disciplining the young man, Hudson blamed the whole thing on the surgeon's sarcastic tongue, causing 'all the ship's company to fall into a rage'. Juet—as easily incensed as ever—walked about the boat muttering that the expedition would end 'in manslaughter, and prove bloody to some'. Juet also began telling people that Greene had been hired by Hudson to spy on the crew, something so palpably untrue that Hudson nearly set Juet ashore in Greenland, but then reconsidered.

Finally, battling icebergs and gales, the *Discovery* found its way to the mouth of Hudson Strait, where the awestruck Prickett described their tiny ship manoeuvring between huge icebergs: 'In this our going between the ice we saw one of the great islands of ice overturn, which was a good warning to us not to come nigh them, nor within their reach … Some of our men this day fell sick. I will not say it was for fear …'

But Prickett leaves the impression that the crew was terrified, with the exception of Henry Hudson, who boldly moved his ship farther down the strait, a 720-kilometre (450-mile) long channel that runs between Baffin Island and the Canadian mainland.

'A Sea to the Westward'

The *Discovery* passed through land that appeared as if it belonged on the dark side of the moon, especially to those crewmen who had explored the verdant Hudson with their ship's captain. Here were forbidding rocky shores, and the only vegetation was weeds and so-called 'scurvy grass', which at least contained anti-scorbutic properties. Hudson began to give islands they encountered names—optimistic names like 'Hold with Hope'—but the crew muttered so much that he at last allowed them to vote to see whether the voyage should be continued. A slim majority said yes, and onward they went until, in early August, they reached a vast open sea. Hudson's last existing journal entry reads: 'Then I observed and found the ship at noon in 61°20' [latitude] and as sea to the westward'.

The sea was, in fact, the great gulf of water that would be called Hudson Bay. Hudson, for the moment, dared to think he had reached the northern Pacific Ocean. Jubilant, he headed south. Jubilant, he did something that he had been probably thinking of doing for some time: he fired Robert Juet, who had been stirring unrest among the crew or, rather, replaced him as first mate with a man named Robert Bylot.

Unfortunately, things did not thereafter go as Hudson wished them to. He sailed south, but by early September reached the confines of James Bay, in the southeastern part of Hudson Bay. Unable to believe that he was not in the Pacific, he began to tack north and south, east and west, repeatedly, 'in a Labyrinth without end', as Prickett wrote. The early northern winter began to set in and 'the nights were long and cold, and the earth was covered with snow'.

Still Hudson sailed on, crossing and re-crossing his own path, and some of the men began to suspect he had gone mad. At last, on 1 November, he brought the ship into James Bay and announced his plans to spend the winter in this desolate spot. They built a crude shelter, but there was very little food and the men began to slowly starve, despite the fact that they were able at first to shoot wild fowl and catch fish. The gunner, John Williams, died within a few weeks, perhaps of scurvy. One lonely trapper of the Cree Indian nation came to them over the winter and Hudson treated him well, but he did not provide them with much food and the men were reduced to eating frogs. With the arrival of spring, birds returned from the south and it was this that saved the crew. With enough rations amassed for two weeks, the *Discovery* set sail in early June, sailing gingerly between the broken ice of James Bay.

Mutiny and Death

As the *Discovery* headed north, Hudson replaced first mate Robert Bylot, with whom he had feuded, with an illiterate and unqualified sailor named John King. This caused a number of the men to mutter that Hudson was going to continue his search for a Northwest Passage, instead of heading home for England. Hudson, for his part, suspected the men of hoarding food and ordered searches of their belongings, something the men hated. The tensions of months now finally exploded into open mutiny, with Robert Juet muttering that 'he would rather be hanged at home than starved abroad'. Led by Juet and Hudson's former friend Henry Greene, the mutineers stormed Hudson's cabin on the morning of 22 June 1611, dragged the protesting master out and put him in the ship's boat along with his son and seven other sailors, most of them sickly. Prickett writes that they gave Hudson supplies, but this may have been written with an eye toward the court of inquiry that was sure to follow. In any event, the intent was certainly to abandon Hudson in an inhospitable wilderness, which was tantamount to killing him. And it did— no one ever saw Hudson, his son or those seven other sailors again.

The *Discovery*, after an arduous voyage, arrived back in England. Conveniently, Hudson's journal had disappeared by that time, probably destroyed by the mutineers. With equal convenience, Robert Juet died a few days before the vessel raised England. One would think, given the fate of other mutineers in British history, that the crew of the *Discovery* would be severely punished but, curiously, this was not the case. Several of the survivors were immediately sent back to Hudson Bay—on the self-same *Discovery*—in order to chart fur-trading routes. They were considered too valuable to hang. Finally, in 1618, seven years after the fact, four of the crew, including Prickett, were tried but acquitted of the crime.

This was partly because Prickett had been successfully able to place most of the blame for the mutiny on Juet and Henry Greene. Greene's fate is quite interesting. As the *Discovery* reached the northeastern tip of Hudson Bay after abandoning Hudson, they stopped and sent a party of men ashore to bargain with Indians they saw—possibly Cree or even Inuit. Something went wrong, somehow, and the Indians attacked them, badly wounding Prickett and killing Henry Greene, along with three others. The survivors barely made it back to the ship. Even without Henry Hudson, it seems to have been the fate of his men to have bloody encounters with native peoples.

CHAPTER SEVEN

Single-minded Pursuit of a Dream
La Salle and the great Mississippi River

During the fierce winter of 1668–69, René-Robert Cavelier, Sieur de la Salle, often sat in front of a blazing fire entertaining guests. Gale-force winds might howl outside, through the tiny settlement of Montreal, Canada, but inside things were comfortable enough, although, had he seen La Salle's guests, Samuel de Champlain, dead some thirty years, would have rolled over in his grave. The men who smoked and laughed by the fire with La Salle were Iroquois Indians of the Seneca tribe, some of the same Indians who had so bedevilled the Huron who had come to Champlain for protection.

These Seneca had arrived in Montreal late that autumn to trade furs but had then stayed on, all through the long Canadian winter, mainly because of the presence of La Salle, who understood Indians. He spoke seven or eight Indian languages and knew how to listen. That winter, he listened very carefully.

These visiting Seneca spent most nights gathered in La Salle's home. They wore breechcloths and leggings made out of deer skin and leather caps with a single feather stuck in the top, and they kept their hair short, although not in the traditional scalp lock or crest down the centre of the head known as the Mohawk, which they saved for times of war. Sitting around La Salle's fire, with bearskins thrown over their shoulders, they told La Salle about a massive river that began three days' journey north of their territory (which was in present-day western New York State) and flowed into a vast sea. The river was so long, the Indians told La Salle, that a man in a canoe would take six or eight months to float down it to the ocean.

The Indians called this river the Ohio—meaning 'beautiful river'—and said that its banks were alive with game, including wild cattle, by which they meant buffalo, and that Indian tribes too numerous to count resided along its mighty flow.

When the Indians left for the evening, La Salle would write down what they had told him and he would begin to dream. It was his dream that this great river flowed into what he knew as the 'Vermillion Sea', the Gulf of California. If this were the case, then he had found a way across the American continent to the Pacific Ocean, a way that would be worth more in trade than all the gold and silver the Spanish hauled out of gold mines in Mexico.

And that, La Salle decided during the long and dark winter nights, was a dream worth pursuing.

A Place of Opportunity

Born to a wealthy and politically connected family in Rouen, France, in 1643, René-Robert Cavelier, Sieur de la Salle (this last referred to the name of the Cavelier estate near Rouen), grew up in wealth and privilege but was an ascetic young man, a fact that makes his transformation into one of North America's greatest explorers even more astounding. He entered the Jesuit order—the most powerful Catholic religious order in France at the time—with the intention of becoming a priest, but, although he was brilliant at his studies, he was also, according to his teachers, stubborn and intractable. While he ended up taking his vows as a Jesuit, he soon renounced them, but this left him with the little problem of what he was going to do with his life. Taking vows in a religious order, even if they were renounced, disqualified a person under French law from inheriting from his family. La Salle thus sailed to New France, where his brother Jean was a Sulpician monk in the new settlement of Montreal (the Sulpician and Recollect friars, both groups part of the Franciscan religious order, would ally themselves with La Salle for his entire life, much to the jealous dismay of the Jesuits).

La Salle arrived in Montreal in 1666 and immediately began seeking his fortune. Montreal was originally established by Champlain in 1611 as a trading post on the St Lawrence River, but the city itself was founded by Sulpician friars, who were only too happy to sell the ambitious young La Salle a large tract of land located along the river some 15 kilometres (9 miles) southwest of Montreal. For the next three years, La Salle set to work clearing the land, building houses and forts and attracting settlers to live there, to work farms or hunt in the surrounding wilderness.

New France at this time was undergoing a sea change. Champlain had founded the colony, but after his death in 1635 little had been done to improve it—as late as 1660 there were only twenty-five settlers in Quebec in any given year, and these had to fight to survive Indian attacks and harsh winters. But now the glorious Sun King, Louis XIV, had finally recognised the importance of a North American empire to rival the one the British were establishing farther south, and he was offering inducements (including women) to get settlers to brave the dangers of the New World. There was a sense that the mainly uncharted wilderness beyond the fragile settlements was a place of opportunity, for those strong enough to grasp it.

In Search of the 'Beautiful River'

In the spring of 1669, after his conversations with the visiting Iroquois, La Salle was determined to find the river they had talked about. He was so obsessed with a passage across America to Asia that scoffers named his little settlement *La Chine*, meaning 'China'—a name for the area that persists to this day—but no amount of ridicule was going to deter La Salle. On 6 July he headed up the St Lawrence River with nine canoes, which carried an assortment of backwoodsmen, Iroquois guides and Sulpician friars, whose goal was to find

Indian tribes that had not yet been converted by the Jesuits.

Like so many explorers at the time, La Salle had no idea of the size of the North American continent or what he was really looking for. The 'Beautiful River' the Seneca were referring to, given where they told La Salle it was located, was probably the Ohio River itself, which flows into the Mississippi (although, confusingly, the Iroquois referred to the Mississippi as the 'Ohio' as well). By 2 August the expedition had reached the easternmost of the Great Lakes, Lake Ontario, which appeared to La Salle 'like a great sea with no land beyond it'. They paddled along the southern shore of the lake until they reached the home of their Seneca guides, a place where most of the Indians had seen few white men. While there was currently a peace treaty with the Iroquois, La Salle knew the Indians enough to be wary of them and thus, while he gave the Seneca trade goods and they feasted him in return, he wanted to be off as soon as possible.

But he needed a guide for this journey farther west and the Indians kept putting off the moment when they were going to provide him with one; this began to concern him. The Iroquois also began to drink some brandy they had received from Dutch traders in the Hudson Valley, after which they would threaten the French mockingly with the very knives the French had given them as gifts. The final straw was when a Shawnee prisoner was brought into the centre of camp and tortured to death in front of the French; the poor man was then dismembered and eaten, with the Iroquois trying to get the French to have a bite or two.

This behaviour seemed so blatantly hostile that La Salle decided to move the expedition along on his own. Guideless, they departed the Seneca village in early September and made their way farther along the southern shore of Lake Ontario. When they got to the western part of the lake, they heard a great roaring sound that was actually the sound of the Niagara River where it pours over Niagara Falls, a huge, 60-metre (200-foot) high waterfall the Seneca had told La Salle about.

The falls were 50 kilometres (30 miles) away, yet their booming noise could be heard on the lake, which impressed La Salle, but not enough to make him deviate from his route to become the first European to see them—that would be Father Louis Hennepin, some years later.

When La Salle's expedition reached the far western end of Lake Ontario, they met a French trapper, Louis Jolliet, who had great familiarity with the region and told La Salle that the way to reach the fabled Mississippi was not to head straight west but to follow the Great Lakes route—Lake Erie to Lake Huron and down around Lake Michigan's coastline to Green Bay or points farther south. La Salle refused to believe he would have to travel that far north to go west, so here, in late September, his group split up. The Sulpicians decided to head north to try to convert the Indians in the Upper Great Lakes, while La Salle moved west with a small group of men and a Shawnee guide he had picked up along the way.

'Empty Dreams and Empty Pockets'

Guided by the Shawnee, La Salle led his canoes along the southern shore of Lake Erie, seeking a water route to the Ohio River. The expedition got lost numerous times in trackless wilderness. Finally, his men abandoned him, slipping away one night and leaving La Salle completely alone. This would have daunted a lesser explorer, but not La Salle, who had an incredible capacity to endure hardship. He went on, alone with his guide, canoeing along the shores of Lake Erie until he found a route to the Allegheny River, which in turn led him to the Ohio. He then headed down the Ohio. Most of the Indians he met had, for the most part, not seen white men, and his encounters with them were part of what made him different from most Europeans. Like Champlain before him, he treated the Indians with respect (although he did not idealise them), and they returned it by providing him with food to supplement the game he caught hunting.

Thus, La Salle travelled along through the wilderness, all the way down the Ohio River to a point, near the present-day city of Louisville, where fierce rapids impeded his progress. Here he decided to return home. Although some historians have claimed that he reached the Mississippi on this solo expedition, it does not appear that he did so, but he became the first to explore the land south of the Great Lakes. At the time, this was small consolation for La Salle. As the historian Donald S. Johnson writes, he returned to *La Chine* 'with empty dreams and empty pockets' late in 1670 and was forced to head out again into the wilderness as a trapper to replenish his depleted coffers.

He had not given up on his dream, but he was soon to receive disappointing news, for in 1673 the same Louis Jolliet he had met along the shores of Lake Ontario—who had advised him to find a Great Lakes route to the Mississippi—had found the great river and travelled down it with the Jesuit Father Jacques Marquette. While they had not gone all the way down to the river's mouth—and while the information they provided actually helped La Salle's own plans—he could feel his opportunity slipping away. He needed to have funding for his great expedition to the Mississippi and began to lobby for it. Making a powerful friend in Count Frontenac, New France's new governor-general, La Salle had himself appointed governor of Fort Frontenac, a new fort and trading post that had been placed in the wilderness at the juncture of the St Lawrence River and Lake Ontario. The furs that flowed into this fort from the west, brought by Iroquois Indians, proved so profitable that La Salle felt he now had a case to make for a government-funded expedition down the Mississippi. And he decided to make the case to the Sun King himself.

'We have Received with Favour'

Returning to France in 1677, La Salle—his skin tanned by years in the wilderness, his long black hair flowing down his back—laid it on thick for the French court. The area west of New France and south of the Great Lakes, he wrote in a petition submitted to a minister of the king, was 'Nearly all so beautiful and so fertile; so free from forests, and so abounding in meadows, brooks and rivers; so abounding in fish, game and venison, that one can find there in plenty and with little trouble, all that is needful for the support of flourishing colonies'. There are even 'native wild cattle', La Salle wrote, obviously referring to buffalo, 'which, instead of hair, have a fine wool that may answer for making cloth and hats'.

On 12 May 1678, La Salle received a reply from the king, which read, in part: 'We have received with favour the very humble petition made us in your name, to permit you to labour at the discovery of the western parts of New France'. The king then conferred on La Salle a five-year monopoly to explore and trade in the Mississippi Valley. It was all La Salle could have hoped for and he headed back for New France in great excitement, despite the fact that the king was not going to actually back the enterprise financially—La Salle would have to raise the money himself, which he did by dint of some wealthy backers.

Once in New France, La Salle began to gather men and supplies for the expedition at Fort Frontenac. He hired as second-in-command an Italian named Henri de Tonty, one of the most colourful characters on the frontier at the time. A Sicilian of good family who affected aristocratic airs, he was a tough-as-nails soldier who had lost his right hand in a grenade explosion fighting in Sicily and thus wore a gloved iron hand in its place.

La Salle also decided that his expedition was going to be too big for canoes, so he commissioned the building of a sailing vessel, the *Griffin*, a 45-tonne barque (a three-masted, square-rigged ship), on the western shores of Lake Ontario, near the mouth of the Niagara River and the roaring of the mighty falls upstream. The builders had to be careful—the Iroquois understood instinctively that such a large vessel represented a quantum leap in the capacities of the French to plunder further the lands to the west—which the Iroquois themselves were beginning to spread into—of the bounty of furs so important to both the whites and the Native Americans.

It appears that the Indians may have twice tried to sabotage the ship during its building.

However, by August 1679 the *Griffin* was finally ready. It was towed up the Niagara to Lake Erie and launched with great ceremony, which included a three-gun salute and a priestly blessing. La Salle was aboard, but just barely—rumours had been spread by his enemies in Montreal and Quebec that his expedition was in bad shape, and many creditors tried to recall their loans. Promising that he would send back furs to them to pay his debts, La Salle set off on the adventure of his lifetime.

Fort Heartbreak

Becoming the first sailing vessel ever to ply the Great Lakes, the *Griffin* headed across Lake Erie, through the Detroit River and Lake St Clair, and into Lake Huron. Sailing north along the lake's stormy shores, the ship arrived at Fort Michimilimack-inac at the juncture where Lake Huron meets Lake Michigan. This important, though squalid, trading post was run by Jesuits, who La Salle discovered to his horror, were out to do him serious damage.

Jealous of the royal patent La Salle had received, the Jesuits were stirring up trouble among the Indian tribes farther to the south, in the Illinois Valley, which La Salle would have to traverse to reach the Mississippi. Not only that, but La Salle had sent men ahead to Fort Michimilimackinac to trade for furs and help prepare for his voyage—these men, it turned out, had squandered his money and goods and had now fled into the wilderness. Sending Tonty after them, La Salle sailed aboard the *Griffin* to the head of Green Bay, on the western side of Lake Michigan. There other men of La Salle's had indeed traded for furs, which La Salle decided to send back to Niagara aboard the *Griffin* to try to assuage his creditors.

La Salle himself then took canoes and paddled with his men and supplies to the southern shore of Lake Michigan, where he waited for Tonty to arrive, for from this agreed-on rendezvous point they would launch their descent of the Mississippi as soon as the *Griffin* rejoined them. Tonty finally joined La Salle in mid-November but, though the expedition waited and waited, there was no sign of the *Griffin*. Deciding he must push on, La Salle led his men through the wintry Midwestern plains south to the land of the Illinois, which they reached in January 1680. At first these Indians welcomed them graciously, but then an agent of the Jesuits reached them from Fort Michimilimackinac and told them that La Salle was secretly in league with their age-old enemies, the Iroquois. The persuasive La Salle denied this and managed to calm the Indians down. Even so, six of his party, afraid of being massacred, deserted, and to calm the rest down La Salle was forced to build a small fort apart from the Indians. He named it Fort Crèvecoeur, or Fort Heartbreak.

This expedition, which was intended to bring La Salle fame and glory, was ending up in bitter disappointment for the French explorer. Chief among his worries was that the *Griffin* was long overdue to return with badly needed supplies. Unable to figure out what had happened to the ship and unable to wait any longer, the extraordinary La Salle set off with a few men on what the historian Francis Parkman called 'the hardest journey ever made by a Frenchman in America'. On 2 March, leaving Tonty in charge of the fort, La Salle took several men and headed back overland to Niagara to discover the fate of his ship.

The journey covered 1600 kilometres (1000 miles) and took them sixty-five days. It was, as Parkman wrote, 'the worst of all seasons' to undertake such a trip, since the sun warmed the snow into a morass of semi-frozen muck at noon, then froze it again at night. The small party traversed the previously unexplored wilds of southern Michigan, pushing through forests so dense that, as La Salle later wrote, 'our faces were so covered with blood that we hardly knew each other'. At one point, they had to outrun a war party of marauding Indians and spent three days hiding in trackless swamps. When they finally reached Niagara, only La Salle and one other man could walk. Two men died of pneumonia shortly after the arduous trek ended.

The Mississippi, at Last

La Salle was nothing if not resilient. By July 1680, he was off again with a new group of men to return to Fort Heartbreak and begin his exploration anew. However, on his way there he discovered that Tonty's men had mutinied and that rampaging Iroquois had destroyed the nearby village of the Illinois—La Salle arrived there on 1 December and found, according to Parkman, 'nothing but signs of fire and the rage of the Iroquois. There remained standing only some charred stakes, showing what had been the extent of the village. Upon most of these stakes the heads of the dead had been affixed to be devoured by the crows'.

Searching desperately for Tonty, La Salle explored farther out into the prairie and found 'the heads and entire bodies of women and children, empaled and roasted and then set up in a field'. There was no sign of Tonty or any survivors of any type. La Salle was forced to winter nearby. However, in June 1681, he received some good news—Tonty, having had a narrow escape from the Iroquois, was safe in Fort Michimilimackinac. The two of them returned to Fort Frontenac, raised an entirely new expedition and in February 1682 at last canoed down the Illinois River and into the great Mississippi. With them, in a flotilla of canoes, were twenty Frenchmen and an equal number of Indians.

Canoeing the Mississippi was an experience La Salle would never forget. It was a dangerous river, especially as spring came on, filled with fast-moving floating objects—ice floes, trees, dead animals. Yet it was a place of great beauty, its wooded banks teeming with animals, low forested hills rising in the distance, other great rivers—the Ohio, the Arkansas, the Missouri—pouring into it, as if all the waters in the world were joined in this one broad stream. Although La Salle took the precaution of camping on islands whenever possible to ward off Indian attack, the French had little trouble with the native peoples they met along the way—the Chickasaw Arkansas, Tensas, Nachez, Coroas and Oumas—with the exception of two incidents. At one point, near the present-day city of Memphis, Tennessee, an expedition member went missing while hunting, but La Salle presented gifts to a nearby tribe of Chickasaw and, while the Indians never admitted taking the man, he soon came floating down the river on a log, nearly starved to death but alive, having been released by his captors. Farther south, they met Choctaw Indians who fired barbed arrows at them from the bank, an invitation to battle that La Salle wisely ignored, keeping his flotilla moving along.

The priests accompanying La Salle's expedition erected crosses wherever they went and held ritual Masses for the Indians. The Indians could not possibly have understood much of what was going on but, according to one priest, 'they showed that they relished what I said, by raising their eyes to heaven and kneeling as if to adore'.

Finally, there were signs they were reaching the ocean—the water had a brackish taste and the shores slowly widened out, going from swamp to sand. At last, on 6 April 1682, they reached the Gulf of Mexico. On a small hillock near the shore, La Salle erected a column with the words: 'Here Reigns Louis the Great, King of France Navarre'. He then made a speech claiming the entire territory for the king.

It was a momentous occasion in the history of New France, and in the life of La Salle—for both the dreams of the country for a territory to rival that of Spain and England, and the dreams of one man for glory were finally fulfilled.

'One of the Greatest Men of His Age'

Following the Mississippi to the Gulf was one thing, but creating a territory there was quite another. With but a short time left on his patent, La Salle headed back up the river and arrived in Quebec by November 1683. But his patron Frontenac had been recalled to France and those in power were unfriendly to La Salle, causing him to take the first ship he could get to France to persuade the king that a colony at the mouth of the Mississippi would be a great boon to France.

In January 1685, La Salle, in command of a fleet of four ships, sailed across the Atlantic and into the Gulf of Mexico, completely bypassing Canada and his enemies there. Unfortunately, taking this unfamiliar route, he was unable to find the mouth of the Mississippi and sailed past it into Texas, into the same bleak regions where Cabeza de Vaca had wandered (see page 73). He finally landed and established a fort, but by the following year two-thirds of his settlers had died of sickness or bites from the many poisonous snakes that inhabited the region.

Desperate, La Salle set off with twenty men to try to find the Mississippi, intending to ascend it and head back to Canada for help, but on 18 March 1687 his men turned on him and murdered him with a single shot to the head. They then stripped him and left his naked body to be eaten by crows. 'Such was the end', said Henri de Tonty, 'of one of the greatest men of his age'.

CHAPTER EIGHT

The Voyage of the Endeavour
James Cook and terra australis incognita

One day late in the fall of 1769, a group of Maori were gathering clams on the shores of a bay they called 'Gentle as a Young Girl', because its waters were so calm. They were on what is today known as the North Island of New Zealand, at a spot now called Mercury Bay. Suddenly, one of their number pointed and shouted. Something very strange had appeared on the ocean. It looked like a bird with giant wings or, some thought, a floating island.

Gradually, the Maori realised that the object was a large ship, far bigger than any they had ever seen. One of those present, a young boy named Te Horeta, lived long enough to be able to recount the story to white listeners in the next century. He said that as this massive ship approached, the Maori elders decided that it had come from the spirit world. This assumption was confirmed when a small boat was lowered from the larger vessel and very pale beings began to row the boat toward shore. They had their backs toward land and so the elders said that they must be goblins of the spirit world, because they were paddling with eyes in the back of their head.

These goblins landed on shore and all the children fled into the woods while the Maori warriors watched warily. The pale spirit creatures seemed to mean them no harm. They gathered clams and oysters. Some of them put flowers and shells in small bags. Gradually, the children filtered out of the woods and came closer. They even dared to touch the goblins. 'We were pleased by the whiteness of their skin and the blue eyes of some of them', Te Horeta recalled. The goblins began to eat the fish and roots the Maori offered them, so perhaps they were not goblins after all. They offered the Maori food in return—fatty meat that Te Horeta thought might be whale meat, but the meat's 'saltiness ripped our throats' so that even the warriors in the clan could not stomach it and spat it out.

One of the goblins pointed a rod in the air and fired a shot out of it and a bird fell out of the sky, which puzzled the Maori—what had killed the bird? A little later some trading was going on and one warrior tried to make off with the coat of a goblin without giving anything in return. The goblin pointed his rod, there was the noise like thunder, and the warrior fell dead, a wide hole in his back. Now the Maori understood that these were weapons.

However, they did not blame the goblins for the warrior's death because he had been, after all, stealing. The goblins stayed in the bay for several days and one day Te Horeta and some others went on their ship. There they met a tall goblin who said little but examined the Maori closely. He patted the boys' heads and gave them small presents. Then he took a piece of charcoal, pointed to the shore and handed it to a Maori elder named Toiawa, who realised that this goblin wanted a sketch of the coast of the land they called Aotearoa, or the Land of the Long White Cloud.

The Maori drew the land for the tall goblin as best he could, including Te Reinga, the cliffs at the tip of the North Island where spirits flew into the next world. Toiawa lay down on the deck and pretended to be dead to illustrate this concept to the goblin—who, after all, should have gotten the point immediately.

However, the goblin did not understand them and finally the Maori left. A short time later, the ship sailed away and the Maori did not see them anymore. But before Te Horeta left the ship, the tall, quiet, kind-seeming goblin patted his cheek and blessed him with a gift: an iron nail, whose use Te Horeta did not understand for some years, but which he treasured as a sacred object for the rest of his life.

'A Noble Man'

The tall goblin Te Horeta was referring to could only have been James Cook for, as Te Horeta said, 'A noble man, one of high standing, cannot be lost in the crowd'. And certainly this greatest of British explorers was also one of the most intelligent and honest men to sail the Pacific Ocean during the great Age of Exploration. While it was his fate, like that of Magellan, to be killed by the indigenous peoples he made contact with, he also treated them far better than most Europeans of his day.

Cook, the son of a Scottish immigrant and farm worker, was born in 1728 in the village of Martonin-Cleveland in England. Despite being born 'inland', as it were, the sea was somehow in young Cook's blood. He was desperate to work on board a vessel, and finally his father agreed that James could apprentice on a coal-carrying ship plying the North Sea. It was tough duty, but the eighteen-year-old Cook loved it. In his spare time, he taught himself mathematics and navigation and was soon appointed as mate.

In 1755 he volunteered for the British Royal Navy during the Seven Years' War and shipped off to North America to fight the French. Here he was instrumental in charting the shoals of the St Lawrence River, going out at night in a small boat, taking depth soundings in pitch darkness as French sentries paced above him on the cliffs of Quebec (where another great Pacific explorer, Louis-Antoine de Bougainville, was stationed). At one point, Cook leaped out of the bow of his boat to save himself from French Indians jumping into the stern to try to kill him. His efforts were credited with allowing the British fleet to safely attack the French stronghold.

Cook's reputation was made by his sterling war service—which included charting lengthy parts of the rugged Canadian coastline—and furthered by his published account of the solar eclipse of 5 August 1766. Although he was still not even a lieutenant in the Royal Navy, he came to the attention of the British Admiralty and the Royal Society of London for the Improvement of Natural Knowledge, generally known as the Royal Society. The Royal Society was planning a grand expedition to the recently discovered island of Tahiti, in the South Pacific, in order to have scientists observe the transit of Venus, a rare but predictable astronomical occurrence in which Venus passes across the face of the sun. Using sightings taken from different parts of the globe, the Royal Society hoped to measure the distance from Earth to the sun.

'A Land of Great Extent'

James Cook finally received his commission as lieutenant for this voyage—the first of what would become three famous journeys of discovery—and set off from England in August 1768 aboard HMS *Endeavour*. The *Endeavour* was no cutting-edge and sleek new vessel, but instead a fat, squat, 360-tonne collier, or coal vessel, which was exactly the type of ship that Cook had cut his sailing teeth on. He had made sure the ship was well fitted for the voyage—with an extra layer of wooden hull to protect against the voracious tropical worms, twenty-two cannon, enough food for a year and extra cabins for all the scientific personnel on board, chief among them the brilliant naturalist Joseph Banks.

At this time, Cook was forty years old, tall, lantern-jawed, bluntly handsome and plain spoken. He was the kind of man who inspired instant trust and who also inspired men to follow him, despite occasional eruptions of temper that sent his officers scurrying away as fast as they could. He was perfect for this job he was publicly given—that of getting the scientists to Tahiti by 3 June 1769—and also for the job that was secretly bestowed upon him: to find *terra australis incognita*, the Unknown Southland, the southern continent that had long been rumoured to exist in the Pacific Ocean somewhere between New Zealand and the South American continent. Scientists speculated that there needed to be a landmass below the Tropic of Capricorn in order to balance out the heavy northern continents of Europe and North America—without one, surely Earth would go spinning off its axis?

European peeks at Tasmania, New Zealand and present-day Western Australia had led people to think that this might be the southern continent, although many others still believed it was farther east and south—that its mountain peaks could even be seen, on clear days, from Tahiti. And so Cook's secret orders, once all the fussing about the transit of Venus was over, were to sail from Tahiti and proceed southward in order to find the 'Land of Great Extent' that some in the British government believed would provide a vast trading market for British goods 'sufficient to maintain the power, dominion, and sovereignty of Britain, by employing all its manufactures and ships'.

Tahiti and West

After stopping briefly in Rio de Janeiro, Cook took the *Endeavour* south, rounding Cape Horn and heading into the Pacific. He landed in Tahiti on 13 April and built a small fort while the scientists readied their instruments to take readings on the transit of Venus in June. Like Bougainville and Samuel Wallis before him, he was greeted enthusiastically by canoes full of shouting and laughing Tahitians offering to trade coconuts and fruit. The crew aboard—some of whom had been with Wallis—were looking forward to the Tahitian women especially, since a single nail from the ship could buy hours worth of pleasure—the Tahitians, as one historian has written, 'valued iron above virtue'. Cook understood this and had brought barrels of extra nails along, although not for trading for women, but for goods and food. Much to his men's dismay, he had drawn up a list of trading 'rules', which made it an offence punishable by flogging to trade for sex with the Tahitian women.

James Cook was a man who liked good order on his ship and knew how to enforce it—at least four seamen were given two dozen lashes with a cat-o'-nine-tails for breaking the rules, but some were punished because they had been harsh with the Tahitians. Many more, no doubt, found a way around the trading rules, although Tahitian women were perhaps not the great beauties they had all heard about—Cook, for one, wrote that he found them 'very masculine', perhaps because the royal princesses among them could weigh as much as 135 kilograms (300 pounds) and stand 1.8 metres (six feet) tall.

The day for the transit of Venus was 3 June and it could not have been more beautiful—hot and cloudless. Two telescopes were set up in the sand, while pieces of smoked glass were passed around so that people could look at the sun. At exactly twenty-one minutes and fifty seconds past 9 am, Venus began its journey across the sun, but the scientists watching saw 'a dusky shade around the body of the planet' that threw off their measurements. (It turned out that this shade was caused by the smearing of the image of Venus by turbulence in the Earth's atmosphere, which instruments in the eighteenth century were unable to correct for.)

While the scientists may have considered their expedition a failure, Cook did not. After bringing on new stores and repairing his vessel, he was off on what he considered to be his true mission: to seek the southern continent.

'We Again Launched Out'

Heading south from Tahiti, Cook found himself among the beautiful, high and hilly islands he called the Society Islands, after the Royal Society. He wandered through these islands for a month, guided by a Tahitian priest named Tupaia, who had begged to come along and who, in fact, proved an able guide and translator. Once they departed from the Society Islands—'we again launched out into the ocean, in search of chance and what Tupaia might direct us to'—they sailed directly, following Admiralty orders, toward 40 degrees south latitude, which was where the southern continent was postulated to be. Two months passed by. Once they hit 40 degrees the weather turned cold and stormy, for they had arrived in the area known to generations of sailors as the 'Roaring Forties' where the wind blows around the southern part of the world without any large landmass to impede it.

'The seas ran mountain-high and tossed the ship upon the waves', wrote one of the scientists present. 'She rolled so much that we could get no rest, or scarcely lie in bed.'

Obviously there was no continent here, so Cook—'we had no prospect of meeting land', he wrote in his journals—now followed his secondary orders to turn west in order to seek the land found by Abel Tasman a century earlier, to see if this was part of a *terra australis*. After about a month or so, they began to see seaweed and driftwood floating by them, a sign that land was near. Excitement ran high and Cook offered a gallon (about 4.5 litres) of rum to the man who first spotted land.

It turned out to be a boy—a twelve-year-old named Nick Young—and he got not only the rum but a coastal bluff (Young Nick's Head) named after him. Cook had arrived on the east coast of New Zealand's North Island. New Zealand is made up of the North Island and the South Island, separated by a strait now known as Cook Strait, and it is one of the most isolated places on Earth, physically speaking, 2000 kilometres (1200 miles) from the nearest continental landmass, Australia. Thus it was one of the last large places on earth to be settled. The general consensus is that the islands were visited by Polynesian travellers in about 800 AD, perhaps drawn by the long white clouds that hang over New Zealand and can be seen far out to sea. The Maori peoples who were the descendants of those Polynesians developed in isolation for 800 years until Abel Tasman showed up and had his bloody encounter with them.

But that had been 127 years before and 500 kilometres (300 miles) away on the western side of the South Island. Not only did Te Horeta not know of this incident but, as Cook later discovered, even the descendants of the murderers at Murderer's Bay had completely forgotten it. So it was really as if Cook had dropped from the sky—no Maori had ever heard of or imagined white men.

'Black Be the Mark On It'

Before meeting Te Horeta's people, Cook and his men had had a far more deadly encounter with the Maori. Upon first sighting Young Nick's Head, Cook had turned south to see if this land—he correctly assumed this was the same land whose west coast had been sighted by Tasman—was possibly connected to a southern continent and was perhaps a peninsula or part of an archipelago.

Within a few days, he ran into trouble. The *Endeavour* anchored off the mouth of a river and Cook went ashore with a few boats to explore the banks of the river. While he did so, four Maori jumped from the woods and ran at one of the sailors guarding the boats; feeling threatened, he shot and killed one of them.

The next day, the British landed again to see the Maori performing a startling dance: 'With a regular jump from the Left to the Right and the Reverse, they brandish'd their Weapons, distorted their

Mouths, Lolling out their Tongues and Turn'd up the Whites of their Eyes', wrote one ship's officer. Clearly, this was not a good thing. The British were seeing a Maori dance called the *haka*, an aggressive ritual performed before any encounter to pump up the warriors' spirits. The Maori were on the other side of the river and Cook, attempting to make peace, threw a nail into the water and then crossed over himself when a Maori warrior waded out to retrieve it.

The men touched noses in a ritual of friendship after Cook laid down his arms, and for a moment there was peace. It turned out that the Maori could easily understand Tupaia's Tahitian language, which differed from theirs only by a few words—both races, after all, had common Polynesian ancestors. Unfortunately, the moment of peace was shattered when a warrior stole a sword and the British shot and killed him.

The other warriors then ran away. Cook, always respectful even when he fought with indigenous peoples, placed beads and other trade goods around the body of the dead Maori, hoping his people would take them as a peace offering. Then he sailed off to another part of the bay—to which he gave the bleak name of Poverty Bay because of his inability to land long enough to replenish his vessel. Here there were seven men fishing from a canoe. Wanting only to scare them away—so that he could land for water and fruit—Cook ordered that his crew fire muskets over their heads. He immediately regretted this. 'Here I was mistaken', he wrote later, 'for they [the Maori] immediately took to their arms, or whatever they had in the boat, and began to attack us'. The enraged or frightened Maori threw rocks, lances and paddles at the *Endeavour* in a brave show of spirit. They even threw their fish at the boat. The British poured musket fire down upon them, killing several.

Cook wrote that night in his journal (in a passage that he later tried to cross out) that: 'I can by no means justify my conduct in attacking and killing the people in this boat who had given me no just provocation and [were] wholly ignorant of my design'. But, he went on, 'when we was once a long side of them we must either have stud to be knocked on the head or else retire and let them gone off in triumph and this last they would of Course have attributed to their own bravery and our timorousness'.

Joseph Banks stated the British regret bluntly: 'Black be the mark for ... the most disagreeable day my life has yet seen', he wrote in his journal.

The Extraordinary Circumnavigation

After leaving Poverty Bay behind, Cook sailed farther southward before reaching a point about 80 kilometres (50 miles) from the southeastern tip of the North Island (something he did not, of course, yet know). With the coast looking bleak and waters boiling up with storms, Cook decided to turn around and head northward. He then engaged on one of the most extraordinary feats of his career—a 4000-kilometre (2500-mile) long counter-clockwise circumnavigation of New Zealand, along rugged coastlines, much of it in the Roaring Forties latitude.

Abel Tasman had only touched at this island. Now Cook was literally going where no European had gone before. The dangers in simply sailing the vessel were manifold—hidden reefs, sudden squalls, sudden shallows and treacherous bays where no anchorage could be found to hold. Once the lee yardarms of the *Endeavour* scraped against the side of a cliff. Yet Cook kept going on his way, patiently sounding shallows with knotted rope and sounding lead, carefully charting what he saw. He generally had better relations with the Maori he now met, as he had with Te Horeta's people, and he was able to gather supplies for his ship, including water, wood, birds and vegetables to treat scurvy. He rounded North Cape in late December (the crew managed to celebrate Christmas in traditional fashion, cooking a fat goose) and headed south along the coast of New Zealand, continuing to chart everything. When the ocean opened up again to his left into a strait 'broad and deep', he intended to make a turn to complete the circle—but then he saw, over the horizon, a blue-green and mountainous mass of land.

Perhaps this was the tip of the southern continent? Cook set out to explore it. He stopped in what he called Queen Charlotte's Sound, on the northern tip of the South Island, a beautiful spot where the crew was allowed to rest and the ship was hauled up and its bottom caulked and patched.

There, on 17 January 1770, Cook came into contact with Maori cannibals: 'Soon after we landed we met with two or three of the natives who not long before must have been regaling themselves upon human flesh, for I got from one of them the bone of the fore arm of a Man or Woman which was quite fresh …'

Cook assessed this in a scientific manner, as did Banks, who even purchased—with a pair of his linen drawers—the head of one of the victims and wrote that 'the flesh and skin were soft but they were somehow preserved so as not to stink at all'. For the rest of the crew it was, nonetheless, frightening. (During Cook's second voyage, ten crewmen from his second ship, the *Adventure*, were killed and eaten by Maoris, and afterwards cannibalism would not be viewed with such detachment.)

More amusing (although offensive to some of the British sailors) was the habit the Maori had of groping the chests and groins of the younger sailors and cabin boys, trying to see if they were women. They could not imagine men travelling without women—in fact, some of the hostility displayed toward the British was because the Maori assumed any group that contained only men had to be a war party. When certain British sailors made signs to the Maori to bring women to them so they could buy sex from them, the Maori brought boys, assuming this was what the British liked.

'I Do Not Believe Any Such Thing Exists'

After resting at Queen Charlotte's Sound, Cook headed east through the strait that now bears his name, and then turned south to circumnavigate the South Island in a clockwise fashion, thus eventually describing a great figure-of-eight around New Zealand. His tour around New Zealand took him six months, but at last he was able to prove, as he wrote, that 'this country, which before now was thought to be part of the imaginary southern continent, consists of Two large Islands'. However, Cook recognised the value of what he had stumbled upon. 'Although it is a hilly, mountainous Country, yet the very hills and mountains are many of them covered with wood, and the Soil of the plains and Valleys appeared to be rich and fertile'.

However, he completely shut the door on the notion that *terra australis incognita* existed to the south: 'As to a Southern Continent, I do not believe that any such thing exists, unless in a high latitude.' Cook now decided to head home (his men, he said, 'were sighing for roast beef'), planning to head west for the Cape of Good Hope. He knew that Van Diemen's Land, discovered by Abel Tasman, was to the west but he was not daunted by the prospect of a large landmass between himself and home. He would simply sail west and see what he found. However, winds drove him a bit north of west, and after nineteen days at sea, on 20 April 1770, he found land. At first he thought this was Van Diemen's Land, but then he realised his error, since Tasman's discovery should have been farther south.

In fact, Cook had become the first European to spy the eastern coast of the continent of Australia. It was a momentous occasion for the British, although Cook did not as yet realise it. He set sail north along the coastline, surveying as he went, until he found Botany Bay (which was first called Stingray Bay for the large numbers of those creatures that could be seen dashing through the waters), so named because of the large number of plant specimens gathered there. In its relatively calm waters, the *Endeavour* anchored and Cook and his scientists and crew went ashore. They spent a few days there collecting specimens and Cook claimed the area for the British crown.

Cook's encounters with the Aboriginal peoples were far less dramatic than the contacts the British had made in New Zealand. As soon as he landed at

Botany Bay, Cook saw 'natives and a few huts' and he approached these people with Tupaia, hoping that the Tahitian could communicate with them as he had with the Maori. But these Aboriginal people were very, very different, and quite strange to the eyes of Cook and his fellows. The British seemed to make little impression on these people they called 'Indians'. Fishermen fished, barely raising their heads to look at what must have been the amazing spectacle of this European vessel. They 'looked at the ship but expressed neither surprise nor concern, to all appearance totally unmoved by us'.

Cook wrote that these people had 'skin the Colour of Wood soot or of a dark Chocolate'. The men had bushy hair and beards and were usually completely naked except for 'White paist or pigment' daubed in thick bands around their foreheads and waists. The women were completely naked. Their huts were poor, their canoes 'the worst I think I ever saw'.

Cook tried to throw nails to the Aboriginals as a peacemaking gesture, but they took it as a threat and one warrior hurled a spear at the British, which caused Cook to respond by shooting a musket loaded with small shot, meant to scare rather than do serious injury. Gradually, the people drifted away, shouting the only words they had spoken— *Warra warra wai*, which the Europeans later found out meant 'Go away'. And, indeed, Cook wrote with some puzzlement, 'all they seemed to want was for us to be gone'. Which they were, within nine days, continuing north and mapping the coastline at a slow pace.

'An Alarming and Terrible Circumstance'

Cook sailed north without a problem for a month or so, until, on the evening of 11 June, near a point that he would call Cape Tribulation—'because here', as he wrote, 'began all our troubles'—shoals were spotted dead ahead. No problem—Cook ordered that the *Endeavour* be pointed farther east, out to sea—to avoid them. There should not have been any problem, because, even though night had fallen, it was a clear one, with good visibility and calm water. But at about 11 pm, the *Endeavour* shuddered and came to a halt with a scraping bang. They had hit a coral reef where, reasonably speaking, there should have been none.

Cook raced up onto deck and began shouting out orders.

We went to work to lighten [the ship] as fast as possible,
which seemed to be the only means we had left to get
her off … throwed over board our guns, Iron and stone
ballast Casks, Hoops, staves, oil Jars, decayed stores,
etc … All this time the Ship made little or no water.

Fifty tonnes of jettisoning later, the *Endeavour* was
still stuck fast and the tide was going out, pushing
it deeper into the sharp coral. The next morning,
12 June, saw the tide rise again, but the ship was
leaking badly, 'an alarming and I may say terrible
circumstance', wrote the horrified Cook, who
loved his *Endeavour* as much as he loved anything
in the world.

Finally, through luck—a piece of the coral broke
off and acted as a plug in the ship's hull, stopping
the leaking—the *Endeavour* was floated off and
taken to the mainland for repair near the mouth
of a river that Cook named after his rescued ship.
He spent seven weeks there, patching the ship up
again and making it seaworthy. During that time,
Cook and his men became the first Europeans to
spot a kangaroo—'except the head and ears, which
I thought was something like a Hare's, it bears no
resemblance to any European Animal I ever saw',

Cook wrote. The local Aboriginal people did show up—this is how Cook knew to call the animal a kangaroo—but became upset that the Europeans were capturing the turtles they themselves regularly hunted in the river and tried to set a fire to scare them off—a situation Cook resolved by firing small shot from his muskets.

The *Endeavour* finally set sail again early in August. Unbeknown to him at the time, Cook had encountered the first signs of the Great Barrier Reef, a treacherous coral maze that extends 2000 kilometres (1250 miles) along the northeastern coast of Australia. As he progressed north, he realised how difficult this maze was. He sought and finally found a passage outside the reefs, but then found himself blown by the trade winds back toward the sharp edge of the coral—'between us and destruction was only a dismal Valley, the breadth of one wave', Cook wrote on one occasion. Finally, however, on 21 August 1770, the ship reached Cape York, the northern tip of Australia, where Cook claimed for Britain the country whose coast he had just traversed: 'I now once more hoisted British Colours and in the name of His Majesty King George the Third, took possession of the whole Eastern Coast … by the name of New South Wales'.

'An Instinct for Discovery'

James Cook made his way back to England by way of the Torres Strait, the Indian Ocean and the Cape of Good Hope. He stopped to provision in the Dutch colony of Batavia, where, tragically, malaria was raging. Ultimately, Cook lost twenty-nine of his men to this disease or dysentery, including several scientists, the talented illustrator Sydney Parkinson, whose sketches captured so much of the voyage, and the adventurous Tahitian, Tupaia. This was especially vexing to Cook, because he had not lost a man to scurvy for the entire voyage, a record at the time. But the *Endeavour* finally returned to England in triumph, arriving on 13 July 1771. Cook had been gone almost four years, had travelled 8000 kilometres (5000 miles) and had made, as he wrote with pardonable pride, a voyage 'as complete as any before made to the South Seas'.

He had not found *terra australis incognita* but had, in fact, explored the real Australia and claimed it for the king. Despite this fact, he was sent back to sea on a second expedition within eighteen months—leaving his poor wife, Elizabeth, behind to care for the five children they had at the time (one more would come later). The Admiralty still wanted Cook to find *terra australis incognita* and this time he navigated the waters near Antarctica, proving conclusively that there was no continent in the southern Pacific. His third voyage, beginning in 1776, took him in search of another chimera, the Northwest Passage, and once again Cook became a man who discovered a great deal while not discovering his goal, for he charted much of the western coast of North America while sailing up into the ice-clogged Bering Strait.

It was on his return voyage that he stopped in Hawaii and was tragically and unexpectedly killed while attempting to regain a ship's boat stolen by natives. In his last journal entry, describing Hawaiians swimming around his ship 'like shoals of fish', Cook wrote: 'We could not help but be struck with the singularity of the scene'. It was the search for such scenes, and such people, that made James Cook one of the most famous men of his age, a man with, as one historian has written, 'that essential quality of all great explorers, an instinct for discovery'.

CHAPTER NINE

First Encounters on the 'Jove-descended Nile'
John Hanning Speke and the quest for the Great River

Of all the great rivers that nineteenth century explorers lusted to explore in Africa, the Nile, even more than the Niger or the Congo, was considered the ultimate prize. The Nile fed the ancient civilisation of Egypt—more than fed it, sustained it—and yet, for thousands of years, no one knew from whence it arose. In the mid-nineteenth century, the source of the Nile was, as one historian has written, 'the greatest geographical secret after the discovery of America'.

It was not as if no one had tried to discover it. The Greek historian Herodotus had travelled up the river a short way around 460 BC, but he had been stopped by waterfalls at Aswan and ended up bringing back only the vague theory that the Nile arose from four fountains deep in Africa. Even the Emperor Nero tried, sending a Roman legion commanded by two centurions, but they found their way blocked by impassable swamps. And it was long known that the shorter Blue Nile (so-called because during the flood season its waters are blue-black), which flows from the southeast, originated in Lake Tana in Ethiopia and joined the main stream at Khartoum—the explorer James Bruce discovered this in the 1770s.

But the source of the White Nile, named for its greyish-white colour, was a deep mystery. It was known it must, of course, originate somewhere to the south, deep within Africa, but the heart of Africa was full of wild tribes who had never seen Europeans and whom no one dared to confront. As far as everyone was concerned, even in the 1850s, the Nile was, as Homer called it, 'Jove-descended', meaning it flowed from the sky.

Burton and Speke

Between 1815 and 1857 many white explorers, mainly British, poured into Africa, the number increasing after quinine was discovered to be effective against the malaria that routinely killed a third of European travellers who entered the region for any length of time. The greatest of these explorers, whose unlikely partnership would result in the discovery of the source of the Nile, were Richard Francis Burton and John Hanning Speke.

Burton, born in England in 1821, was the son of a wealthy ex-army officer. He was probably one of the most brilliant Britons of the nineteenth century, a linguist who mastered thirty languages and was fluent in many others. After an unsteady stay at Oxford (where he considered that he was far too bright for his fellow students, an attitude they naturally resented), Burton joined the army and went to India for eight years, where he perfected his linguistic skills, particularly in Arabic. At the age of thirty-two, he undertook the adventure that made him famous—disguising himself as a devout Muslim pilgrim, he made the *haj*, or pilgrimage to Mecca, claiming to be the first European to do so.

While resting from his journey in Cairo, Burton met a missionary who had been to East Africa and who had barely escaped with his life from the tribes of the region. Burton listened to his stories but, far from being discouraged, formulated a plan to penetrate that region in search of the 'fountains of the Nile'. To toughen himself up for such an undertaking, he decided to take an expedition into Somaliland (present-day Ethiopia) in 1854. When one of the members died before the expedition set forth, Burton consented to take along a British army lieutenant on leave, one John Hanning Speke.

Speke, at twenty-seven years old, was some six years younger than Burton and a very different personality indeed. Born to an old English family, he was tall, with blue eyes and a pale complexion, and had an air of seemingly imperturbable calm about him. He was far from an intellectual and had none of the questing intelligence of Burton— in fact, Speke's main love in life was hunting, especially up and down the Himalayas. On furlough from his regiment, Speke travelled with the idea of undertaking a two-year hunting expedition in the mysterious Mountains of the Moon (the modern Ruwenzori Mountains) in central Africa, where legend had it that the Nile arose.

Speke joined Burton's expedition to Somaliland (although Burton went off on his own for much of it) and they were together at their camp on the coast when Somali tribesmen attacked one night at midnight and a furious fight began. In fighting them off, Burton was stabbed through the left cheek with a spear, thereafter carrying a jagged scar; Speke was wounded some twelve times and captured, although he managed to escape. Despite the fact that Speke would claim that Burton accused him of cowardice during the fight, the two agreed to join in a further, epic exploration of Africa two years later: a concerted search for the source of the Nile.

The Wondrous Lakes

Burton and Speke landed in Zanzibar—the island, some 30 kilometres (20 miles) off the African coast, from whence all expeditions set forth in those days—in late December 1856 and set about raising a team of some 154 men, necessary to carry their supplies and because the desertion rate was so high. Burton and Speke landed on the African mainland in June of 1857 and followed an Arab slaver caravan route that stretched through the flat scrubland of the coast and then wound its way up onto Africa's central plateau. They were heading toward some rumoured lakes—three of them, at least—from which they felt the Nile might arise.

Burton and Speke were already entering territory few Europeans had ever visited and their men were heavily armed with muskets and cavalry sabres. The local inhabitants flocked to see these men with their strange white skin, making such a nuisance of themselves (at least from Burton's point of view) that he wrote a sardonic entry in his memoirs that detailed the twelve different types of stares he received.

Theirs was not an easy journey. Although they possessed quinine, figuring out just how much to take was an inexact science and Burton and Speke both became ill with malaria and recurrent fever. Some disease of the eye blinded Speke, at least temporarily, while Burton suffered from ulcerated legs. As the expedition climbed into the mountains, they were so weak that they often had to be dragged up by their men. To make matters worse, as they got farther and farther into the interior, more and more men began to desert, afraid of hostile tribes. But, at last, on 13 February 1868, they climbed a hill and saw a huge lake before them—or at least Burton saw it, since Speke was nearly blind. 'The whole scene suddenly burst upon my view', Burton wrote, 'filling me with admiration, wonder and delight ... An expanse of the lightest and softest blue, in breadth varying from 30 to 35 miles [50 to 55 kilometres] ... truly it was a revel for the soul'.

Burton and Speke had become the first Europeans to look upon Lake Tanganyika, which Burton was almost instantly convinced was the source of the Nile, although Speke had his doubts. The two men journeyed in canoes partway around the shore of the lake, but fear of hostile tribes kept them from circumnavigating it (this would have to wait for Henry Morton Stanley's expedition a decade later). Instead, the two returned overland to the caravan village of Tabora, to rest before heading back to the coast.

'I No Longer Felt Any Doubt'

After their arduous expedition together, the differences between the two men were becoming more and more pronounced. Speke was a hunter—almost anything else bored him. Burton, who was head of the expedition, disliked Speke going off to hunt because it wasted time but could himself sit for hours chatting with Arab traders, while Speke paced restlessly and resentfully. Burton was intellectually curious to the point of absurdity (at one point he lived with thirty monkeys in order to try to put together a monkey vocabulary) but was also a racist when it came to Africans, especially, writing page after page about their supposed laziness, drunkenness and stupidity.

Speke disliked books and had no such intellectual curiosity, but he was not inclined to be harsh in his judgements about the native peoples he was meeting. Although he had none of Burton's stunning arrogance or extraordinary appearance—Burton, with his jagged red scar and glittering black eyes, made people think of the devil—he was nonetheless his equal in ego. Burton wrote—accurately though bitingly—that beneath his 'modest aspect' Speke possessed 'an immense fund of self-esteem, so carefully concealed, however, that none of his intimates suspected its existence'.

As Burton tarried in Tabora, chatting with Arab traders, Speke grew more and more impatient. He finally proposed to Burton that he, Speke, should go off on a sort of side expedition—a 'flying trip'—to the north, where he had heard rumours of a lake even larger than Lake Tanganyika: the Nyanza, about three weeks' journey away. Burton, heartily sick of Speke, told him to go ahead. This, as it turned out, was a crucial, even life-changing, mistake on Burton's part.

Speke set off with a small group on 10 July 1858. Three weeks later, he stood on the shores of a vast lake, obviously larger than Lake Tanganyika, a lake 'so broad you cannot see across it', Speke wrote, 'and so long that nobody knew its length'. With the lake breeze blowing in his hair, standing on a beach of yellow sand, Speke was stricken with an intuitive certainty 'that the lake at my feet gave birth to that interesting river, the source of which has been the subject of so much speculation, and the object of so many explorers'.

The Nile, in other words. 'I no longer felt any doubt', Speke added. Spending only three days at the lake—which he named Victoria, after the queen—he turned and headed back to Tabora. When he told Richard Burton of his find, Burton wrote scathingly (and jealously) in his journal: 'We had scarcely … breakfasted [upon Speke's return] before he announced to me the startling fact that he had discovered the sources of the Nile … The fortunate discoverer's conviction was strong; his reasons were weak'.

Speke, for his part, wrote that Burton grumpily listened to him and did not contradict him outright, although he could see that Burton was not happy with this news. 'Burton is one of those men', Speke later wrote, 'who never *can* be wrong, and will never acknowledge an error'.

With that breakfast, a famous feud had begun.

'Always Eager to Kill Something'

Speke returned to England two weeks ahead of Burton and immediately went to the Royal Geographical Society to tell them of his find. His enthusiasm so excited Sir Roderick Murchison, president of the society, that Murchison agreed to fund a return trip to Africa so that Speke might further explore his find. When Burton arrived in London, he protested in vain that Speke and he had agreed not to speak to the society until Burton showed up (something Speke denied). By once again letting Speke go ahead of him, he had become the odd man out.

In April of 1860 Speke journeyed to Africa once again, this time to prove the certainty that he intuitively felt. He took with him as second-in-command Captain James Grant, a capable but self-effacing man who was about as un-Richard Burton-like as he could get—exactly what Speke wanted. Speke's plan was to find the outlet river that he was sure ran from Lake Victoria and would flow into the Nile, and then go down it. He arranged for John Petherick, an ivory trader and British vice-consul at Khartoum, to come up the river and meet him with supplies as he descended.

Speke followed his previous route—from Zanzibar to Tabora and then north to Lake Victoria—and when he arrived he set about fully exploring the region that is now Uganda. He was the first white man to do so. Arabs had penetrated south close to the shores of what would become Lake Albert and Lake Victoria, but they had been turned back by Bunyoro people who lived north of Lake Victoria. To the south, right around the northern shores of Lake Victoria, was the fearsome empire of Buganda, and on the western shore of the lake were the Karagwe people, who were quasi-vassals of the Bugandans.

When Speke and Grant arrived in this territory, they were, therefore, forging new ground in encountering the native peoples. Speke, whose eyes still bothered him, wore grey-tinted glasses but had to take them off because they so astonished the tribespeople he met that they were constantly peering into his face to look at them. Speke headed around the western side of the lake first. Without Burton present, there were no checks on his hunting. As he wrote in his journal: '… always eager to kill something, either for science or the pot, I killed a bicornis rhinoceros … and I also shot a bitch fox. This was rather tame sport, but the next day I had better fun'—at which point he recounts killing numerous buffalo during a hunt that he initiated, simply wading in among the beasts and shooting them. Finally, however, he got to Karagwe, on a pleasant plateau filled with open country that gently sloped down toward the lake. He was welcomed by Rumanika, the king, and feasted royally, and then wrote about some of the strange customs of the land—customs that titillated Speke's Victorian readers when he published his *Journal of the Discovery of the Source of the Nile*, but also scandalised them.

Speke wrote that obesity was much prized in Karagwe, and the royal princesses were force-fed to the point where they could no longer walk but could barely crawl along on all fours through their huts. Speke decided that he wanted to measure one young woman and was given permission as long as he showed her the flesh of his arms and legs—unlike his face, which was burned by the sun, his limbs were startlingly white and thus an object of great curiosity. In any event, Speke got the woman to 'sidle and wriggle into the middle of the hut', then took her dimensions—her bust was 132 centimetres (52 inches), each thigh 79 centimetres (31 inches).

The Land of Mtesa

Since James Grant was now unable to walk because of an ulcerated leg, Speke decided to go off on his own northward around the lake shore to the kingdom of Buganda, which was the most powerful and advanced kingdom around Lake Victoria. The houses of the Bugandans were 15 metres (50 feet) high, conical structures made of woven reed or cane. Music filled the air from drums and flutes and trumpets, and Bugandan warriors travelled in elaborately carved war canoes, some of them as much as 20 metres (70 feet) long. Most of the men dressed, according to Speke, 'like prophets of the Old Testament' or ancient Romans, with long togas tied with a knot at the shoulder and white sandals. Noblemen often draped capes made of brushed antelope over their shoulders. Food was plentiful—fish, meat, chicken, sweet potatoes and maize—coffee beans were chewed as digestives and *pombe*, the African banana beer, was drunk plentifully by both men and women.

The ruler of all of this, as Speke arrived, was one King Mtesa, a twenty-five-year-old tyrant with great, liquid dark eyes and a stiff-legged walk that was meant to imitate that of a lion. When Speke was first summoned to the royal court, he found out later, the king's advisors were telling Mtesa to kill him—surely, with his white skin, Speke was a sorcerer. But Mtesa was curious to have the white man around for a while, and thus we have a fascinating image of a long-vanished kingdom in its first encounter with European civilisation.

What stands out most is the cruelty. The punishment for almost *anything*—from forgetting to wear your sandals at court to touching the king's body—was death. While Speke was there, he got used to seeing summary executions every day. One day a girl spoke too loudly in the king's presence; she was dragged off screaming to have her head chopped off (with the pounding of drums masking the actual moment). Attending Mtesa's court (a daily compulsory occurrence) was dangerous for his subjects. Cowardly soldiers were sentenced to be castrated, 'drilled with a red hot iron, until they are men no more'. Other culprits, Speke wrote—'perhaps guilty of showing an inch of naked leg whilst squatting' before Mtesa—might find themselves drowned, burned alive or mutilated. If a particularly prized minister of Mtesa died, the king often sentenced the man's wives to be buried alive with him.

Speke witnessed all this and much more, but he only raised his hand once, to stop the execution of a young girl who had accidentally touched the king while handing him a piece of fruit. Speke was criticised for this when his memoirs came out but, in fact, there is almost nothing he could have done to stop most of these executions. However, he can be faulted for giving Mtesa a rifle as a present—the first firearm the king had seen. Naturally, Mtesa was delighted, as Speke reports:

The King now loaded one of the carbines I had given him with his own hands, and giving it full-cock to a

page, told him to go out and shoot a man in the outer
court: which was no sooner accomplished than the little
urchin returned to announce his success, with a look
of glee as one would see on the face of a boy who had
robbed a bird's nest … The King said to him: 'Did you
do it well?' 'Oh, yes, capitally.' He spoke the truth, no
doubt, for he dared not have trifled with the king: but
the affair created hardly any interest. I never heard, and
there appeared no curiosity to know, what individual
human being the urchin had deprived of his life.

'Old Father Nile'

James Grant, finally healed, showed up in Mtesa's court in July of 1862, and ten days later Speke and he moved out, heading east, where they had heard that a mighty river flowed out of Lake Victoria. But before he left, Speke created further scandal—for Victorians, that is—by accepting the gift of two young girls from the Bugandan queen mother. Speke had an odd relationship with this woman. In her mid-forties and greatly overweight, she held many parties in her huge house, during some of which she was so drunk she had to drink her *pombe* on all fours out of a wooden trough. She complained of stomach and liver ailments; Speke dosed her with quinine, but also sensibly told her she should quit drinking so much, advice she ignored.

However, she was quite curious as to what the children of Speke and a Bugandan girl might look like, and sent the young women over to Speke to 'carry his water', as he writes euphemistically (Speke is the king of indirection in his journals, even referring to his own trousers by the Victorian euphemism 'unmentionables'). Speke appears to hint that he had sex with the girls and then passed them on to his head porters, and this part of the journal angered many of his readers—it was taken for granted that men might dally in foreign climes, but writing about it made one a 'cad'. However, several modern historians feel that Speke was a repressed homosexual who had no interest in the women and was merely writing as he did in order to appear a red-blooded male.

In any event, he and Grant now began to close in on the river that flowed out of Lake Victoria. Before they got there, Speke sent the loyal Grant off on a side mission of little importance—it is apparent that he wanted to be the lone one to discover where the Nile began flowing. And on 28 July 1862, he found it, a waterfall pouring into a wide river:

*Here at last I stood on the brink of the Nile; most
beautiful was the scene and nothing could surpass it.
It was the very perfection of the kind of effect aimed at
in a highly developed park: with a magnificent stream,
600 to 700 yards [600 to 700 metres] wide, dotted with
islets and rocks … I saw that old Father Nile, without
any doubt rises in the Victoria Nyanza and, as I had
foretold, that lake is the great source of the holy river
which cradled the first expounder of our religious belief.*

By which he meant Moses. In a rather telling
moment, he told one or two of his men that they
should 'shave their heads and bathe in the holy
river, the cradle of Moses', but one of them replied
that, since he was a Muslim, 'we don't look on these
things in the same fanciful manner as you do'.

Fanciful manner or no, it was time to move on.
Speke named the falls Ripon Falls, after the well-
known British politician George Robinson Ripon.
With Grant rejoining him, the two men made their
way down the Nile, finally arriving at the trading
village where they were supposed to rendezvous
with Petherick. In fact, Petherick was not there,
which angered Grant mightily, but Samuel Baker
and his wife, Florence, who had been forging their

way up the Nile, were. Baker was disappointed that Speke had arrived before him but was happy to set off in search of another great lake Speke had heard about, the lake Baker would name Lake Albert.

'The Nile is Settled!'

Speke and Grant arrived back in London in 1863, Speke having first sent a famous telegram: 'The Nile is settled!' Of course, this only enraged supporters of Richard Burton, and Speke further angered the Royal Geographical Society (which, after all, had sponsored his expedition) by refusing to publish his results in their journal, since it might interfere with commercial publication of his journals. When he finally showed his topographical figures, he was ridiculed because—sloppy in his calculations—he had the Nile River running uphill.

Finally, in 1864, it was agreed that a debate between Burton and Speke might settle the matter, once and for all, but on the day before it was to happen, Speke died mysteriously. Still, Speke, it would turn out, was correct about the headwaters of the Nile and would go down in history as the first European to view them. He was not a pleasant man—great explorers seldom are—but he was right.

CHAPTER TEN

The Blank Spot on the Map
Mick Leahy prospects New Guinea

Michael J. Leahy—but everyone called him 'Mick'—had a love for unknown wild places bred into him from a very early age. Born in 1901 in Toowoomba, in the Australian state of Queensland, he was the fourth of nine children of Irish immigrants. The family did not have much money, but Mick had a happy childhood wandering the hills of the Great Dividing Range, the mountains that dominate eastern Australia's landscape.

'The blue haze of distance over the scrub-covered ranges towards the coast always fascinated me', he wrote in his classic book *Explorations into Highland New Guinea*. 'With barefooted friends and a few dogs, we hunted wallabies and hares and trapped the small, beautifully marked finches that abounded … My experience fuelled my enthusiasm and my urge to see what was on the other side of the haze-shrouded ranges.' He would soon have his chance.

After leaving school, Mick worked for a time as a clerk with the Queensland Railways, but soon found this indoor job restricting and quit to roam the forests of the eastern slopes of the ranges, cutting timber for railway sleepers. One day in 1926, as he was hauling wood blocks to the sawmill in a Model T Ford truck, he heard the news that there was a gold strike in New Guinea. 'I left my truck by the side of the road', Leahy wrote, 'teamed up with a group of men who, like myself, knew nothing about gold mining or about the country into which we were so impulsively heading, and caught the first steamer to New Guinea'.

The Blank Spot on the Map

New Guinea is the second largest island in the world—only Greenland is larger—roughly 2500 kilometres (1500 miles) from end to end, the distance from London to Moscow, although not quite so civilised a journey. The island has more mountains per square kilometre than any country in the world—a spine of rugged peaks runs the entire length of New Guinea, topping out at 4500 metres (15,000 feet). Areas of these central highlands are known to aviators as 'broken-bottle country' because, from the air, the chalky cliffs appear like the shards of huge bottles smashed into the landscape. Some peaks are snow-capped and there are active volcanoes. Clouds enshroud the deep valleys etched down from these mountains by fast-moving rivers.

New Guinea is a country that holds its secrets well. Settled for at least 40,000 years, it was only discovered by Europeans in 1526, when a Spanish sea captain sailed by and named it *ihas dos Papuas—papuas* from the Malaysian word for 'frizzy-haired', after the natives' wild hair styles. A subsequent Spaniard called the island New Guinea because the islanders reminded him of natives from Africa's Guinea coast, but in fact the inhabitants of New Guinea are unlike any others, divided into numerous warring tribes without any of the inherited chieftainships or hierarchies usually found in such peoples. Instead, power went to those who displayed what social anthropologists call 'aggressive individualism'.

No one got too close to New Guinea for centuries: the terrain was rough and the natives unpredictable—headhunting and cannibalism were endemic there. But by the late nineteenth century, Europeans had decided to carve up the island, which had gradually become a strategic pawn in the ever-expanding world power game of nation against nation. The western half (now Indonesian territory) was owned by the Netherlands, while the eastern half was divided between Germany, in the north, and Britain, in the south. After Germany's defeat in World War I, both the eastern territories were administered by Australia, with the northern part known as the Mandated Territory and the south as Papua.

A map of New Guinea from the early twentieth century shows a well-defined coastline and numerous river systems, like branching trees, but all of these precisely etched lines simply stop as they approach the centre of the island, where there is a massive blank spot. Sometimes such blank spots on maps were marked 'Uncharted' or 'Unexplored', but more often they were simply left empty. Throughout the nineteenth and early twentieth centuries, blank spots had disappeared from maps of Africa, North and South America, the Arctic and Australia, but the tantalising emptiness at the centre of the map of New Guinea remained.

Gradually, in the 1920s, gold prospectors began to mine the country's swift rivers, getting closer and closer to the unknown territories in the country's central highlands—a place, as Mick Leahy wrote, that was considered to be 'a jumbled mass of unpopulated, timber-covered mountain ranges'. His first major expedition, in 1930, would drastically change that perception.

'Very Hungry Spirits'

By 1930, Leahy had been in New Guinea for four years and had not yet struck it rich—the wealthy Edie Creek mines, a walk of some eight days from the northeast coast of the country, were crowded with miners trying their luck. Determined to find 'another Edie Creek', Leahy set off on 24 May 1930 with another prospector, Michael Dwyer, and a group of sixteen New Guinean porters, to head up the Ramu River from the north coast. They had heard rumours of gold inland from solitary miners. Soon they arrived at the foothills of the Bismarck Range that bisects northern Papua New Guinea but found, to their surprise, that they had difficulties finding local guides to take them over the mountains—that people were terrified of being attacked by strange tribes who lived on the other side.

Leahy eventually found an old man who would guide them to the top of the range. From there, he reported an astonishing sight in what should have been an empty wilderness: 'From a small clearing we gazed into a vast area of steep, timber-topped, grass-covered ranges and high mountain peaks. There were fenced gardens in straight rows and smoke curling up from barricaded villages'. This was certainly not a 'blank spot' on a map. Leahy and Dwyer and their men bedded down somewhat uneasily that night and the next day made contact with natives who had never seen white men before. 'We found that first contact with whites was always quite a shock to the natives. They gave no thought to [offering us] food until they saw us picking up pieces of sugarcane and sweet potato skins, when they seem to have realized that although we were spirits of some of their dead relatives, we were also very hungry spirits.'

The natives Leahy met were covered with pig grease, wore string belts but little else, and carried huge shields and bows and quivers of cane arrows.

They pierced their noses in as many as five places, filling the holes with pieces of bone, pig tusk and quartz. This weight caused, as Leahy wrote, 'a continual snuffling' noise, quite noticeable when dozens of natives were present. After getting over their surprise, these people gave the expedition food in return for trade goods, especially steel knives and axes. Leahy and his men set off in canoes they had brought and reconstructed, paddling along the Ramu—here a fast-moving stream 1500 metres (5000 feet) above sea level that runs through steep, grassy hills and then out into a vast open valley populated by 'thousands of Stone Age natives living in barricaded villages with compact gardens nearby'. These tribes were constantly warring with each other, but the appearance of the expedition was so astonishing that they often stopped fighting and flocked to see the white men.

After two weeks of travel, as the river continued and widened, Leahy and Dwyer realised that they were, in fact, no longer on the Ramu (which should have narrowed to its upland source) but on a completely new and undiscovered river, heading downstream through a land that flickered at night with thousands of fires. The natives they met, wrote

Leahy, 'endowed us with supernatural powers and associations', but Leahy also noted that this sense of awe only lasted so long and then the tribes they met began to show an unseemly interest in the fabulous belongings of the white men. Leahy was only too aware that, as far as the New Guineans knew, they were unarmed—they carried no bows, only their guns, which the tribes took to be mere sticks.

'The Most Treacherous Cannibals'

Leahy had entered this country for a limited journey, but this new river was sweeping them along at a rapid clip and he felt woefully unprepared, especially with only two .12 gauge shotguns, two .22 rifles, two .32 rifles and two .45 pistols. He felt that if the party turned back the way they had come, that the natives would have time to get over their superstitions and possibly attack—and that would be a fight the expedition could not win.

It was indeed a savage country. The natives often buried their dead sitting up, with their heads above ground. The dead of enemy tribes, however, were either eaten or left to rot on the ground. Body after body floated down the river, victims of tribal wars higher in the mountains; when they washed up on the sandy banks, giant iguanas came out from the jungle to tear at their putrid flesh. But, without really knowing it, Leahy and Dwyer had become the first Europeans to cross the highland divide in Papua New Guinea. Exhausted, they left the river—which turned out to be the Purari—and made their way down from the mountains to Port Romily, on the Gulf of Papua. Leahy and Dwyer had revealed a country teeming with heretofore unknown people and Leahy, for one, could not wait to go back.

Early in 1931, Leahy was hired by a company called New Guinea Goldfields Ltd to explore the headwaters of the Watut River, which flows through the northern slopes of the Owen Stanley Range. This time he was better prepared. He hired a small plane to take him over the country into which he was going to be walking, to check out the population and to look for flat, grassy areas where landing strips could be built so that the expedition could be resupplied by air (no strips existed in the rugged, mountainous territories).

On 24 March the expedition set off. Leahy had again brought along Michael Dwyer, as well as his own brother Pat and numerous native bearers. They walked along spiny, wooded ridges in the northern part of the Owen Stanleys, through territory whose indigenous peoples, the Kukakukas, had never seen white people before. 'The Kukakukas', Leahy wrote, 'have established a reputation for being the most treacherous cannibals in New Guinea and are said to stalk the ingredients of their meals with the same impersonal single-mindedness that a cat shows in pursuit of a mouse'.

Leahy, his brother Pat and Dwyer, as well as their terrified bearers, were themselves followed by the Kukakukas, who would crowd closely around them until Leahy got in the habit of stringing fishing line around their camps and refusing to let anyone come through it. Things were not helped any when the expedition came upon the empty camp of a German prospector, Helmuth Baum, who had preceded Leahy into the region. When Leahy decided to follow Baum's trail, they were stopped by Kukakukas, who kept making the strange gesture of bowing their heads and pouring water over their necks. Leahy took this to mean there was an impassable waterfall ahead, and turned back. Still, this bothered him, as it should have— for he found out only later that the Kukakukas had attacked, killed and eaten Baum: the strange gesture was meant to show that the German had been beheaded.

Leahy did not know this when he camped a short time later and, therefore, he did not keep as close a watch as he should have. Just before dawn, a commotion broke out—shots were fired and he could hear his porters yelling and screaming. Leahy grabbed his .45 and ran outside into the dim light. A black man was standing a short distance away from him and Leahy thought he was a porter. 'Where are the bastards?' he said to him. Simultaneously, he turned and saw a Kukakuka warrior crossing a stream not 10 metres (30 feet) away. He fired with his .45 and then the world exploded around him. When he regained consciousness he was lying on the ground, with blood pouring down his head. The man he had spoken to was a Kukakuka, who had brained him with his stone 'pineapple' club. Leahy's life had been saved by a porter, armed with a bow and arrow, who had shot the warrior as he moved in to administer the *coup de grâce*.

Leahy could barely see, but he finished out the battle leaning against a tree and firing at the shadowy figures who flitted through the woods near the camp. When the battle was over, he went to check on his brother, who had received two arrow wounds, one to the chest, but had pulled out the arrows and kept on fighting. After this, the wounded expedition staggered back to civilisation, where Leahy learned the story of Baum's death and learned, as well, that the bush pilot with whom he had overflown the territory had died in a plane crash, his severed head rolling down onto a mountain trail where it was found by some hunters.

Sobered by these experiences, Leahy would never underestimate New Guinea again.

'Undisguised Awe and Terror'

In 1932 Leahy returned to the bush, this time to the New Guinea highlands, to an inland area called Bena Bena, which contained tribes of the same name. He brought with him his eighteen-year-old brother Dan, as well as a geologist from New Guinea Goldfields Ltd. Much better prepared this time, Leahy was able to stake several gold claims and cut out an airstrip that was used in the future both by colonial administration officials—who were beginning to take more of an interest in the area now that so many thousands of people had been found—and by gold miners.

Now something of an 'old pro' at first contact, Leahy wrote the following:

*First contact usually elicits undisguised awe and terror
... followed by stunned silence and tears, dances of
what appeared to be joy, and loud, windy speeches by
stone-axe-wielding old men who eventually give all
and sundry their visions of the encounter.*

At this point food would be given to the expedition—the omnipresent pigs, sweet potatoes, sugarcane and bananas—and some serious trading would go on, with these inland people bargaining fiercely for discarded cans and bottles, empty rifle cartridges, even the coloured labels from food tins. 'The natives considered anything associated with our party to be impregnated with the spirits and magic that apparently protected us as we travelled amongst their neighbours and hereditary enemies.'

However, if the expedition stayed too long in any one place, the local people began to covet their possessions. Leahy punished even minor incidents of theft by threatening to shoot the miscreants, feeling he could not show the slightest weakness. In his memoir, it is clear that he feels justified in doing so, and calls the tribes treacherous for their attacks on his party and for their ongoing attempts to steal the expedition's stores—but Leahy had a frankly old-fashioned and somewhat racist mindset when it came to the indigenous peoples he met in New Guinea. He never seems to have asked himself what he might do, back home in Australia, if a large party of heavily armed black men had camped out on the property that had been in his family for centuries, spending a good deal of time scooping dirt from streams and examining it closely.

'We Shall Surely Die'

In March 1933 Leahy and his brother Dan made an expedition into the area around Mount Hagen and discovered the huge and heavily populated Waghi Valley. Leahy and his party hiked into this previously unexplored area, which was full of people 'who had never seen or heard of white skins before'. The people were fascinated by anything having to do with the white men, including their two dogs, from whom they plucked hairs until the animals howled, and also including the animals' faeces, which the locals took home rolled in leaves for leisurely examination around the fireside.

Despite the civilised-seeming nature of their cultivated landscape, Leahy understood that these people were at constant war with each other. Every house had a secret escape tunnel, and Leahy passed numerous burnt-out villages. Refugee groups wandered the land; with no one to take them in, they lived a life of near-starvation in the forests.

Despite some of his attitudes toward the people he met, Leahy understood that he was making history and was careful to make a record of it for posterity. He took over five thousand 35-mm still photographs and several hours of 16-mm movies during the course of his journeys through the backcountry of New Guinea. These pictures provide us with an invaluable peek into a Stone Age way of life just as it was about to change—we can see the cultivated Waghi Valley, with its fenced-in gardens and straight pathways, the warriors with their greenstone axes and the woman who wears her late husband's jawbone around her neck as a sign of mourning.

For their part, the people did not know what to make of Leahy and his group. Anthropologists in the Mount Hagen area many years later asked those who had first seen Leahy's plane fly over what they had thought, and they replied that they had told each other: 'If we look at this thing, we shall surely die'. They gathered closer when he carved out a simple grass landing strip for resupply planes to land, but when the plane came in they would throw themselves on the ground in terror.

Working with Jim Taylor, an official of the Australian colonial administration, Leahy and his brother Pat began to open up others of the hidden mountain valleys in Papua New Guinea—the land of the Goroka, Chimbu and Wabag. Each time, they were the first white men into the valley. 'People could not decide', Leahy wrote, 'whether to laugh or cry' when they saw him. There was only one more attempt at an attack, with an enraged warrior throwing a spear into the camp to signal a massacre, but Leahy put a stop to this by stopping the charging warrior dead in his tracks with two soft-nosed bullets.

'Our Principal Interest in Life'

The strange thing for Mick Leahy was that he never did find any gold—in fact, by 1935 it began to seem almost beside the point. Once, staring from a ridge into unknown country, Leahy reflected that he would have been 'mortified to have a new gold field stop us up before we had a look beyond the ranges in front of us'.

A hunger for contact and new people was what was driving Leahy, not gold. He made a final expedition in 1934 and then a quick foray into the bush in early 1935 to find the killers of a missionary he had befriended, but by that time the Fox brothers, Tom and Jack, had gone all the way to the border of Dutch New Guinea without finding any gold. 'When we heard this,' Leahy wrote, 'Danny and I walked back to the base camp in almost total silence, both of us feeling that we had been robbed of our principal interest in life'. With no evidence of gold, Mick's ventures into the backcountry would no longer be underwritten by companies seeking to mine the precious ore, and he would no longer be able to explore new vistas.

For the next five years, Mick Leahy prospected for gold in areas he had already discovered, but he found very little. In 1935, enraged that colonial administrators were claiming they had discovered the source of the Purari River in mountains Mick and Michael Dwyer had explored on their first journey, Leahy flew to London, where he forced the Royal Geographical Society to hold a hearing so could defend his claims. He was so convincing that the society awarded him its prestigious Murchison Grant and published his reports.

In 1940 Leahy got married and settled down on the New Guinea frontier, just in time for the Japanese invasion during World War II. After his wife was evacuated, he melted into the New Guinea highlands and helped a group of European refugees be airlifted from the Mount Hagen area. He then went to work for the United States Fifth Air Force, pinpointing sites for bomber fields in the wilds of New Guinea.

Leahy lived until 1979, a respected although sometimes controversial figure. While his expedition was not as bloody as those of Jack Hides or the Fox brothers, many excoriated him for his willingness to shoot to kill. Others believed that he shot only when necessary.

Leahy himself held the opinion that he and his men had survived for three reasons: 'Our presumed magic, our superior mentality, and our firearms, in that order'. What no one could doubt was Leahy's bravery and the fact that he had opened up for the world one of the least known places on Earth.

INDEX

ACKNOWLEDGEMENTS

Magnus Magnusson, Herman Palsson © Penguin Classics 1978.
Rolena Adorno, Patrick Charles Pautz *The Narrative of Cabeza de Vaca* ©
    University of Nebraska Press 2003.
Michael J Leahy, Douglas E Jones *Explorations into highland New Guinea,
    1930-1935* © University of Alabama Press 1991.

First published in 2011 by Pier 9, an imprint of Murdoch Books Pty Limited

Murdoch Books Australia
Pier 8/9, 23 Hickson Road
Millers Point NSW 2000
Phone: +61 (0) 2 8220 2000
Fax: +61 (0) 2 8220 2558
www.murdochbooks.com.au

Murdoch Books UK Limited
Erico House, 6th Floor North
93/99 Upper Richmond Road
Putney, London SW15 2TG
Phone: +44 (0) 20 8785 5995
Fax: +44 (0) 20 8785 5985
www.murdochbooks.co.uk

Publisher: Diana Hill
Project Manager: Emma Hutchinson
Editor: Christine Eslick
Design Concept: Jenny Grigg
Design Layout: Helen Beard

Text and design copyright © Murdoch Books Pty Limited 2011
Text first published in *First Encounters* by Joseph Cummins (Pier 9, 2009)

Every reasonable effort has been made to trace the owners of copyright materials in this book, but in some instances this has proven impossible. The author(s) and publisher will be glad to receive information leading to more complete acknowledgements in subsequent printings of the book and in the meantime extend their apologies for any omissions.

National Library of Australia Cataloguing-in-Publication Data:

Author:	Cummins, Joseph.
Title:	Journeys of discovery : momentous expeditions that expanded the world / Joseph Cummins.
ISBN:	9781742662336 (pbk.)
Series:	Pocket history.
Notes:	Includes index.
Subjects:	Discoveries in geography.
Dewey Number:	910.9

A catalogue record for this book is available from the British Library.

Printed by Hang Tai Printing Company Limited, China.